When Memories Come Calling

Tom McDonald

Published by:
Bluewater Publications

www.BluewaterPublications.com

If you can find a truly good wife,

she is worth more than precious gems!

Proverbs 31: 10

This book is dedicated to my wife, Margo. She has been the rock in my life for almost fifty years of marriage.   In late summer of 1964, she agreed to marry me while we sat in the parking lot at the Hardee's restaurant near O'Neal Bridge, where I was working and earning eighty-five cents an hour. She graciously accepted the engagement ring containing a microscopic, teeny-weeny sliver of diamond.   In return, I received a gem far more valuable than I could have ever imagined at the time.

The illustrations for this book, except the one on page 127, were provided by Jackie Hastings of Belmont, Mississippi. Jackie is an ordained minister who loves his family, music, art, and, especially, his Lord Jesus Christ.

Contents

Introduction 1

Daddy's Peach Tree 3

Older Brothers 6

The Piano 11

Empty Grave 15

Boys, Bikes, Wagons and Trains 17

Mountains and Mopeds 22

Church Cat 29

Pa Mac 31

Milking 38

Paperboy 42

Brandon School Memories 47

Road Trips 54

Children and Church 61

My Favorite Aunt 63

Like Father, Like Son 67

Whistlers 69

Charm School 71

George, the Donkey 75

Teachers 78

Front Porches and Fireplaces 85

Growing Old Together 91

Is That All? 97

Beavers or Beepers 101

Promises We Make 105

East Florence Playgrounds 109

County Fair 113

Cars 117

Olden Times 120

Up On the Roof 125

Sorry About That 127

Swimming Holes and Boys 131

The Last Switchback 134

Fighters and Floggers.. 138

Surplus Roosters and Raccoons 143

What Could Have Been 147

T'was the Day after Christmas 149

Some Embarrassing Moments 153

Driving Jaybo 157

Blessings, Campfires and Dulcimers 161

Fire Trucks and Orange Crush... 165

Economics 101.. 169

Desperate Measures 174

What Color is that?... 177

Introduction

On more than one occasion, I have heard it suggested that an event of some significance caused someone to, "turn over in their grave." If this actually happens, my Freshman Comp instructor will be in a perpetual roll when she discovers I have written a book. Writing a book was never in my thought process because people who write books have to do massive amounts of research, make notes on 3 X 5 index cards, assemble the morass of information into something legible and provide footnotes to prove it was not all made up. I began some thirty years ago by simply writing a few stories about my childhood in case my children ever showed any interest. One can gauge their level of severe boredom by the amount of sighing and eye rolling observed. Children are rarely enthralled by their parent's stories about growing up until they are well into their own adult years. Unfortunately, by then it is sometimes too late. My intention was to prove to our children that their parents actually had a life before they were born. It seemed important they know something about their parents, grandparents and great-grandparents. Children and grandchildren should know about the length of the journey, not just the last few steps. Over the years I made volumes of notes on ideas which I thought might someday turn into a story. They were written on napkins, envelopes and scraps of paper which were handy at the time. As my wife cleaned out desk drawers and cabinets, many of the original notes resurfaced. When I sat down and tried to remember the thoughts that had inspired the notes, my memory frequently failed me and many of them were not productive. The remaining notes, and other observations, turned into this book. It took a lot of soul-searching on my part before making the final decision as to whether or not to go forward with the publication of this book. The words came easy enough but that was not my problem. It was the feelings that scared me. The exposure of my private feelings to the scrutiny and possible ridicule of others has been far more frightening than I would have ever realized.

This miracle would not have taken place without the insistence and support of my wife, Margo. For some reason, she thought those little stories might be worth saving and possibly enjoyed by others. At least, on this one occasion, I sincerely hope she is right and my pessimism goes down in flames. Naturally, I took advantage of the author's prerogative to rearrange and refurbish facts to my advantage when necessary to move the story forward. Hopefully, reading this book will not turn you against reading, or against me.

Daddy's Peach Tree

While cutting grass the other day, I had considerable trouble mowing around some peach trees. I was particularly aggravated because they were in my way and wondered why in the world those trees were planted in that part of the yard. Sometimes I question if they are worth the time and trouble it takes to avoid them with the lawn mower. They are not very large but two of them began to bear for the first time this spring. The fruit from one of them, while still very small, was as tasty as any I have ever eaten. It seems every time I get to thinking about doing away with them, I think of another peach tree planted in the same general area. Then I remembered the current trees were planted to be close to the little peach tree which has long since disappeared. I always called it Daddy's peach tree. When he was living in the trailer by our old house, he saved the seeds from some delicious peaches someone brought him from Athens. For some reason, peaches from the orchards near Athens always seem to be sweeter and juicier than any we grew ourselves. He was never one to throw anything away, not even a peach seed. The seeds were planted in one of the little flower boxes on his front porch. Dad's very last piece of carpentry work was to construct these two boxes. He built them in my shop and labored over them a long time. His hands were no longer steady and it was very difficult for him to stand for any length of time. I wanted to step in and help him but I knew this was something he wanted to complete by himself. That dogged determination to finish got him through many a rough time in his life. He persevered through times so difficult that many men would have given up and melted away into the night unable to face the hard times. My daddy passed on a lot of good traits to his children and one of the most valuable was to never give up. So, he didn't give up on the flower boxes and hung on until they were finished. I saved the boxes and still have them although they have just about rotted away. Anyway, he watered and weeded the seeds religiously. I just thought it gave him something to do with his time. Most folks would never have seen anything develop, but, as Dad had a way of doing, he was successful in coaxing one of the seeds to sprout. The little sprout prospered under his gentle touch and, after he went to the nursing home, Margo and I continued to look after it. Eventually his trailer was sold and I put the tree in a larger container and replanted it in a flower bed when it was large enough to survive outdoors. This was about the time we were looking to move and the house at Central was sold and we moved into a rental house in town while building our current home. The peach tree was dug up and moved to town with us where, much to my surprise, it continued to flourish.

The little migrant tree was moved once again when our new house was completed and one of my first priorities was to get it in the ground. This was the fall of 1991. The tree never missed a beat. The next spring saw it produce leaves and it grew rapidly. To protect the delicate trunk from lawn mowers, gnawing rabbits and other critters, I drove stakes around it and wrapped it with stiff wire. The tree produced buds and leaves again the next spring and experienced another season of growth. We were beginning to look forward to eating some of the fruit, as we were certain it would soon begin to bear. But, more important than any fruit it would ever produce, the little peach tree provided me with a living memory of Daddy. I never failed to think of him when I saw the tree.

I don't think I've ever mentioned this to anyone, but the reason I have always kept dogwoods trees in my yard is because Momma loved dogwoods so much. When we first moved to the country, she sent me out every winter to dig up a dogwood and plant it in her front yard. My fumbling efforts were always in vain because none of the transplanted trees ever lived. She would watch the tree eagerly in the spring, searching the branches for buds, but none ever appeared. I am sure I damaged the roots while digging them up and didn't know enough about what I was doing for them to have

The author's father, W. E. McDonald on his front porch. The wood planter, which sprouted the peach seed is to his right.

a chance. Neither of us realized the difficulty in moving a large dogwood tree. So I guess the peach tree and dogwoods in our yard were living reminders of both Momma and Daddy.

Daddy's peach tree was seemingly doing great as late as Saturday, April 16, 1994. However, early on the morning of April 18th, I noticed all its leaves were wrinkled and brown. As far as I could tell, Daddy's peach tree died on April 17, 1994, the same day our brother Dan passed away. The tree had not previously been injured or harmed in any way. The leaves did not wilt or show any signs of distress until the very day it expired. All of a sudden, and for no apparent reason, the tree just suddenly died.

I am not a sentimental person and not generally prone to speculate on the reason things happen. I just sort of plod along and accept whatever comes my way. Trying to decipher why things happen the way they do is beyond me. A more learned person could surely explain in scientific terms about the demise of the peach tree. Maybe it had something to do with the acidity or the alkalinity of the soil. Maybe it was the victim of a fast acting disease or didn't get enough moisture. Who knows? I have always thought it was a blessing that Daddy passed away before any of his children. He loved all of us more than life itself and would not have been able to bear the burden of losing a child. Maybe, just maybe, his sorrow did find a way to express itself.

Older Brothers

My parents had seven children, of which I am the youngest. Out of the seven, six were boys. We often told people who asked about the size of our family there were six boys and each one had a sister. This led to huge misunderstandings about the size of our family.   A neighbor once pointed at a duck and said it wasn't really a duck but was actually a stork whose legs were worn short from delivering babies to our house. Since I was very young at the time and not really up to snuff on the birds and bees thing, it sounded sort of logical.   A passel of older brothers relieved my father of his duty to sit down and explain the facts of life to me but they left a lot of gaps and I grew up not sure about a lot of things.

Numerous studies have been done by experts that attempt to explain certain personality types based on birth order within a family.   For example, an only child behaves a certain way because it receives 100% of its parent's love and attention and grows up not having to share anything with siblings. Middle of the pack children have a different behavior pattern than those siblings born before them and those born later. Some say the youngest of a large brood is often the most unpredictable. They don't know which way to go and who to emulate and frequently go off on unexplained tangents.   The majority of people incarcerated in prisons and mental institutions probably fall into this group. My parents knew nothing of this study but it might have helped them to better understand what was wrong with me.

Brothers at the wedding of Joe's granddaughter. From left; Bill, Joe, John, Tom and Bobby.

I was always extremely proud to have so many older siblings. Many of them left home during my early childhood but their visits were occasions to celebrate. Those times always meant good food and a lot of stories a young boy could repeat to his buddies. Some of these stories may have actually been true, but, considering the source, I have my doubts. It was very special when one of my brothers in the Navy returned home on leave. I was usually the recipient of another white navy cap and some prize brought back from ports across the ocean. Two of my brothers were in the midst of a career in the Navy. Our daddy wanted me to do the same because he couldn't imagine retiring after only twenty years with a pension and free medical care for the rest of your life. His mother died when he was only three years old and he had to drop out of school in the sixth grade and work with his daddy, who was a jack-leg itinerant carpenter. He worked like a crazy man to support his family until he was sixty-five and retired from TVA as a carpenter foreman. I loved my brothers deeply but I couldn't see myself following in any of their footsteps. It was always a joyful time at home on these occasions until our mother smelled liquor on one of her sons and the mood darkened considerably, but she always cried when they left to go back.

Older brothers were also the source of words not normally known to the unsophisticated illiterates in my own age group. Information of a more bawdy nature could be had by listening carefully as older brothers confided with their colleagues about the girls who wore tight short-shorts. It was extremely important for the younger brother to know which of these new words could not be used in the presence of an inquisitive parent, who always asked, "Where did you hear that word?" A misspoken word could spell doom for an older sibling. There was an unfortunate incident during which I unknowingly created quite a bad situation for my brother Johnny. We

Parents of the McDonald Clan, Ervin and Pauline.

were responsible for creating our own entertainment in those days and occasionally we just sort of snooped around until something interesting turned up. One day we uncovered some unused pieces of ceramic tile like that found in a bathroom. It had been discarded but presented some great possibilities for a bunch of boys. Several ideas were considered but discarded. Finally, one of my brother's older friends suggested we scratch code words on the surface of the tile with our pocket knives. There was no mention of what the code words would be used for but it seemed to evolve around confusing any foreign spies who might be in the neighborhood. The idea had a lot of merit and everyone began scratching away. I was too young to read or spell and did not know any good words to write so I simply copied the code word that my brother's friend had already scratched on his piece of tile. Unfortunately, it was a four letter word that every parent lives in fear of hearing their child utter. The other boys hid what they had written so that the spies would not be able to get their hands on our secret code. I was very proud of what was probably the first word I had ever written so I put my piece of tile in my pocket to show my parents. When we sat down to eat supper that evening the tile was proudly displayed right beside my plate. Johnny was seated on the other side of the table and saw my grievous mistake but realized he would attract too much attention by trying to get to it before it was too late. His efforts would have done no good because an audible gasp from our mother brought the situation to a head rather quickly. Our daddy always ate standing up and had to be summoned to the table to view his youngest son's handiwork. A rattlesnake on the table would have attracted less attention. Daddy realized anyone brainless enough to be proud of something like what he was seeing on his kitchen table was too stupid to understand the severity of the situation and turned his attention to my brother for an explanation. Johnny quickly gathered his thoughts and offered a clarification which would have made a defense attorney proud. Unfortunately, he was arguing his case before a hanging judge who had a reputation for swift and sure punishment. My relationship with my brother was strained for a few days but older brothers forget quickly and don't carry a grudge.

A lot of older brothers provided a host of tangible and useful benefits, some which only the youngest can fully appreciate. As a kid, I was always short and scrawny, definitely at a distinct disadvantage in the scuffles that always occur among boys. Put a bunch of boys together and before long there will be a fight. If challenged, one had to fight because it was a matter of pride and acceptance by the pack. The fight could be sparked by any one of a number of factors too numerous to mention. There was one thing that saved me from more than one beating. It was commonplace back then for older brothers to take up for their younger ones. They were allowed to beat up on their younger brothers, but other boys did not necessarily have the same privilege, especially if they were older and larger. It was a generally accepted rule that if you couldn't whip the oldest and strongest, you shouldn't mess with the youngest and weakest. Knowing this, I wisely made sure, from early on, that everyone was fully aware of how many older brothers I had who would exact a terrible vengeance on anyone foolish enough to beat up on me. Hindsight tells s me that my sister should have been a part of this threat. She was enough of a tomboy to whip just about any of the guys in our neighborhood. Besides, the humiliation of being beaten up by a girl would have probably made me a lot safer. At that time, this type of information was circulated chiefly by word of mouth. If Facebook had only been available my safety would have been assured.

Older brothers from left, Bobby, Joe and Dan.

However, being the youngest of a large group of siblings has a downside. In the natural order of things, one would expect the oldest to pass away first, leaving the youngest for last. This exact sequence has not been followed in our family, but four of my brothers are now gone. As we grow older, we sort of accept the inevitable mortality of our aging parents. The death of an elderly parent is not completely unexpected, most of the time. For me, the gradual loss of my brothers has been more painful than I could ever have imagined. To watch helplessly as these idols of my boyhood gradually succumbed to the ravages of sickness is a fate I would not wish on anyone. Even years after the fact, it still seems unreal. There is no doubt that sister siblings share a similar bond that others don't understand but that is a topic on which I am not qualified to render an opinion. I do know, without a doubt, that brothers share a bond that is unique. My brothers and I have shared things over the years that we did not share with anyone, even our spouse. These things have not been deep, dark secrets but instead, brotherly advice about not making the same mistakes they did and about dreams that died without ever reaching fruition. Older brothers seem to be born with the obligation to give advice to their younger brothers, even to the very end. As we die, each of these shared moments will die with us because you would have had to have been there for it to make sense.

Rarely a day goes by that something, and it could be most anything, does not occur that reminds me of at least one of my brothers. These recollections sometimes bring a tear, but more often a smile, or even outright laughter.

The McDonald children with their father. From left; Dan, Bill, W. E. McDonald, Johnny, Virginia, Joe and Bobby. Tom kneeling in front.

The Piano

Most homes probably contain one or two items that have much more sentimental value than market value. They are generally passed from one generation of the family to the next. Over time, these items become priceless to people inside the family circle who are aware of their history, while others are more than ready to send them to the flea market. The piano, which sat in our living room for many years, fits this description. One of my earliest memories is the day the piano arrived at our old house. It is puzzling that I can remember something like a one time delivery of a piano over fifty years ago and cannot remember my wife's birthday which comes around on a yearly basis. The price of a new piano in the mid 1950's was probably a fraction of what one would cost today but, regardless of the cost, it had to be a struggle for Daddy to afford the payments. In my memory, it was the only time he ever bought something brand new for the house until long after all his children were married. After the delivery men struggled with it down the hill and managed to squeeze it through the front door, it became an object of great sentimental value to our family probably because it has always been a direct link to our mother. The piano had a shiny, sleek finish which made all of the other old furniture in the house pale in comparison. But its appearance was the least of its virtues. When my mother took her seat on the stool and began playing the old gospel hymns she loved so dearly, the entire house seemed to stop and listen. My mother played the piano by ear, at least, that was the way it was described to me. In other words, she never had a lesson in her entire life but could play a song after just listening to it. That was a good thing because there was no way my daddy would have been able to pay someone to teach her to play. In the scheme of life, the ability to play any musical instrument without the benefit of lessons seems grossly unfair. Many of us spend countless agonizing hours practicing in a futile attempt to just reach a level of basic competence while those who play by ear can learn a song by listening to the radio. But those who grieve over the unfairness of life face a lifetime of suffering.

As far as I know, my mother never played for a crowd of any kind. When the mood struck her, she would just sit and play and anyone within hearing distance would be her audience. She was an extremely quiet and shy lady who never sought the spotlight in any situation. From the perspective of her youngest son, she never put on airs, never spent money on fancy clothes and never learned to drive a car. Her life was devoted to her family as she never held a job outside her home. Raising six boys and a girl, while caring for a live-in father-in-law and her youngest sister, were sufficient to occupy all her time. Her house was lacking in all of the conveniences we take for granted today but she

11

always managed to get by with what was available. I remember watching her heat water on the kitchen stove and pour in the bathtub for us to have a hot bath and watched her boil our clothes in a black kettle in the back yard so her children could be presentable in public.

We sweltered in the summer with only a window fan to kidnap an occasional breeze and shivered in the winter with only a coal stove to heat an entire house. The arrival of the piano in her house was something she had dreamed of for a long, long, time but it had to take its place behind other, more essential items. Replacing the coal burning stove in the living room with a gas furnace had a much higher priority. Those who have never lived in a house whose only source of heat in the winter was something burning in a fire place or in a pot-bellied stove will never appreciate the luxury afforded by a gas furnace which made the whole house warm in a matter of minutes. However, it did take me a while to learn not to step on the hot furnace grill in the middle of the house because it left my bare feet branded on the bottom with a perfect grid pattern. Having branded feet was a no-brainer because that meant my brother and I would no longer have to pick up pieces of coal left on the tracks when the train was unloaded at the coal yard. Our daddy couldn't see the coal going to waste so we took our empty burlap sacks down the hill to the tracks behind the coal yard, as our older brothers had done before us, and filled them to the point we couldn't carry them back to the house. We had to sit beside them and wait for Daddy to arrive with his car; otherwise they would have been taken by a more enterprising person who saw a sack already full of coal as an opportunity to avoid some heavy labor. This was a classic case of the early bird getting the worm.

The last major hurdle to clear before the piano became a reality was the hot water heater, which eliminated having to heat the bath water on the kitchen stove. It is difficult to prioritize such things, but having gallons of hot water instantly available by simply turning a faucet has to be close to the top of the list. Replacing the window fan with an air conditioner was apparently a low priority for Daddy because I never lived in an air conditioned house until long after I was married.

My mother passed along this amazing gift to play by ear to my sister who used this talent to entertain others for many years. While our mother was shy and avoided attention of any kind, our sister inherited the other set of genes. To paraphrase a passage from the Bible, where two or three are gathered you will always find my sister, is not meant to be critical. As a matter of fact, it is actually a compliment because she has more friends and knows more people than all her brothers combined. She was blessed with such an out-going personality her brothers often wondered if maybe she was adopted. But, on the other hand, God never created a more loving and kind-hearted person. Her love for her brothers has never been in question in spite of being on the receiving end of far too many practical jokes at our hands. It was her misfortune to be stuck with a bunch of brothers who loved her dearly but considered it unmanly to tell her so. Thank goodness, we finally became mature enough to realize how silly we had been. She said many times she always wanted a younger sister and I have always suspected that I was the brother she would have willingly traded to make her wish come true. Being the only girl with six brothers could not have been easy but she survived and it made her a better person. That is not to say she did not seek a lot of sympathy for her plight, but her whining fell on deaf ears.   The brothers all called her Sis, for obvious reasons, and this name soon caught on and everyone who knew her, aunts, uncles, nieces, nephews, cousins, classmates, friends, neighbors, called her Sis, instead of Virginia, her given name. Even today, it is easy to determine who knew her growing up by the name they use when referring to her. To the best of my memory, I have never called her Virginia.

The piano stayed in our living room, even after Sis married and moved out. It followed us to our home in the country and remained there until our mother passed away. Daddy donated it to Pleasant Hill Church under the stipulation that it be returned to the family when a new one was purchased. The piano remained in the church sanctuary for about twenty years before being replaced. During that time it played countless Methodist hymns, consoled grieving families at funerals and sent many a newly married couple skipping out the church doors to a lifetime of wedded bliss.   My mother would have been proud. The piano now resides in the home of one of my sister's grandchildren, and that is where it should be.

Empty Grave

Many times, while hiking in the Great Smoky Mountain National Park, I have passed cemeteries deep in the woods. Most are very small with only a few graves and can be easily passed by unseen. At one time they were probably well kept with loved ones visiting frequently that knew exactly who was buried in each site, even if the grave was not marked.   One thing all these cemeteries had in common was that they contained the graves of many infants. The presence of these infant graves in large numbers only adds more proof that life was very difficult in the mountains. There is something very sad about an abandoned cemetery with unmarked graves of people who have essentially been forgotten. Such a sight often left me wondering about the people buried there, their lives, where they came from and how they came to rest in such a place.

My oldest brother had a lifelong pursuit of researching and recording family history.   A lot of his information was obtained by talking exhaustively with older family members, even when he was very young.   They repeated to him stories passed down to them by their older relatives of the long, grueling trek they had to endure to arrive in this area. They told of family members who died along the way and were buried in forgotten graves alongside a trail they would never see again. He wrote down their stories and kept meticulous records.   He studied census reports and courthouse recordings of marriages and deeds. Before their death, many relatives insisted that he accompany them to barely remembered graveyards so they could point out the resting place of long dead relatives so that someone would know their final resting place. Some of these were actual cemeteries and others were lonely burial spots in pastures and wooded areas.   A few were marked by rocks and a few by headstones but many were not. He kept extensive records and vowed to eventually erect markers on these graves. This was accomplished by soliciting assistance from family, mostly younger brothers, to help purchase and erect these markers. Being the youngest, and most available, I accompanied him many times to forsaken places and placed markers on the graves of a lot of people I did not know.   We carried the heavy granite markers up steep hillsides, along with bags of cement to secure them in the ground. If the area was grown up, we carried axes and chainsaws to clear the brush away from gravesites. While we rested, he would talk about the person whose gravesite we were clearing. The stories he had gleaned from his conversations with older relatives years back gave some meaning to what we were doing. At one time, these folks walked, talked, slept, ate, had dreams and lived their allotted time on this earth before they died and were placed in the ground.   Sometimes we tend to think the world didn't begin until the day we were born and everything before that time had little meaning. I learned from my brother that the eyes of some of the men in the graves we were marking had seen and been a part of events we only knew about from history books. One had been at Valley Forge and undoubtedly had seen George Washington many times. Another fought in the pivotal battle at Cowpens which helped turn the tide of the Revolutionary War toward the newly created United States of America. Others had fought at a bloody place called Shiloh and later marched with General Jackson in the Shenandoah Valley campaign. Some of these men may have fought for causes that are unpopular today but their lives were anything but insignificant. These conversations with my brother helped me to come to grips with who I was in the continuum of the history of our family and I began to realize why he considered it to be important for their mortal lives to be remembered in some small way. They were real people with real lives much like our own except they lived in a different time.

I have many fond memories of these trips and one thing I will always remember is that every one of those graves contained the remains, bones or dust, of a human being who departed this earth. They eventually suffered the same fate that awaits all of us, they died. The story of their life has already been written and their destination for eternity rests in the hands of the One who defied death and the grave. I know of only one truly empty tomb. Jesus Christ, our Lord and Savior walked out of his tomb and arose to sit at the right hand of God. There could be no greater news for mankind than the fact that his TOMB IS EMPTY! We do not worship a man name Mohammed or Buddha whose bones are still in the grave. We worship a God who is alive and is calling us to come and spend eternity with him, although it may be from abandoned and long forgotten graves, when our time on earth is over.

Boys, Bikes, Wagons and Trains

The author on the back porch of the family home in East Florence.

Psychologists tell us that parents should recognize and accept the fact that it is important their children be given opportunities to become independent over a period of time. As parents it is very difficult to let go of our children and allow them the opportunity to experience the hard knocks the world has for them outside the security of home. The bonds holding us to our parents should be loosened slowly as the child gets older. In other words, kids have to get out from behind their mother's skirt sooner rather than later and flex their wings like a bird leaving the nest. Parents are not doing their children a favor by sheltering them from every possibility of hurt and harm. Otherwise, gaining full independence as an adult will never fully take place and this can result in major problems down the road.

One of the most liberating events from my early boyhood occurred when the old bicycle that all my older siblings had used finally became available for me to use. Learning to ride a bike in our family was sort of a rite of passage from being just a kid to being a real boy. Of course, the next step in this progression in the coming years is for the boy to get his first car and then finally become a man, at least to his way of thinking. The irony that I had to go through this first rite to manhood on a girls' bike escaped me at the time. How it came to make its home with our family was never a topic of discussion, but one thing is absolutely sure, it didn't come straight to us from some store. The old bike was made entirely from aluminum, scraped and dented beyond repair but the fact that it had no cross bar like those on a boys' bike made it easier for my short legs to reach the pedals. The chain guard was long gone and presented a major annoyance. The lack of this necessary part caused my right pants leg to constantly catch between the chain and the sprocket, thereby immobilizing the bike until it was removed, which was not always an easy task. This was usually accomplished by hopping alongside the bike on my left leg while simultaneously moving the pedal in reverse until the bottom of my pants was ejected from between the two pieces of metal. The fact that I never see a kid today in the same predicament causes me to believe that this problem has been pretty much solved with new generation bikes. Another major flaw with the bike was that the brakes would not work, which made it difficult to ride a long distance since we lived on the top of a steep hill. This was not a recent development with the bike because the brakes had never worked, at least as long as the bike had been in the possession of my family. One of my older brothers was baited into accepting a double-dog dare and foolishly rode this very bike, with no brakes, down the notoriously steep Nichols hill. To his credit he had a plan, but it was a bad plan. His scheme was to hurdle the railroad track at the bottom of the hill and allow the waters of Sweetwater Creek to bring him slowly to a halt. Unfortunately, in his haste, he forgot about the deep drainage ditch which ran parallel to Sweetwater Avenue, a major obstacle he had to cross before reaching the tracks. The story goes that the head first plunge knocked him unconscious and as he lay there in the bottom of the ditch a passing lady motorist, stopping to render aid, looked at him and proclaimed he would be all right because he was, " one of those McDonald boys and everybody knows you can't kill them." An ironic aside to this story is that the boy lying bruised and battered in the ditch grew up to marry the niece of this lady and she became, "Aunt Bessie" to a new generation of McDonald children. Since this was my oldest brother and he survived on the bike, I suppose our daddy's thinking was it would not be fair to allow all the other kids to learn to ride on a bike with brakes. So, for the next several years, I rode the bike while ascending the hills in the neighborhood and on whatever flat ground I could find but had to push the bike down the descents. Frankly, this took a lot of joy out of the process because everybody knows that going downhill is the fun part of any bike ride. When I grew old enough to be embarrassed by having to ride a girls' bike, my daddy did relent and buy me one that was much safer; it had brakes that worked.

The presence of so many hills in our neighborhood gave birth to another scheme that was sort of kamikaze-like but, fortunately, with a higher survival rate. We began racing homemade wagons down these hills and around corners at break neck speed, again with no brakes. It was up to each racer to design, build and drive his wagon, which was quite a challenge. The key element, of course, was in obtaining wheels in sufficient numbers that were the right size and durable enough to hold up under extreme conditions. It was not a difficult task to scavenge individual wheels but the problem was in finding two wheels that matched to the point they were at least the same diameter as its mate on the opposite side of the same axle. It was desirable for the rear wheels to be larger than those in front because it made the wagon look like it was always headed downhill and, to our wrong-headed way of thinking this would make it run much faster. Once we had the wheels in hand, the project was off and running. Scrapping together enough lumber for my wagon was never a problem for me because my daddy was a carpenter and always had lumber in his shop. He was generous enough with his scrap pieces of lumber but not so generous with his tools. A blood oath was necessary for me to put them back where I found them before he allowed them out of his shop. Basically, the materials list consisted of a few pieces of wood, preferably 2 X 4's, a short piece of rope and two axles the same diameter as the hole in the center of each wheel. The main chassis of the wagon was a 2 X 4 about five to six feet long. A shorter piece of lumber about three feet long, centered and nailed at right angles to the chassis, provided the support for the rear axle and wheels. The front axle was shorter than the rear and it was attached to a 2 X 4 that had a hole bored in the center to match up with a hole bored in the front end of the chassis. These two pieces were loosely connected with a bolt which allowed the front axle to turn. The rope was nailed to each end of the front axle and extended back to the seat and this provided the steering mechanism. A foot rest in front of the seat was the final piece of this primitive engineering marvel.

The downhill runs available could be lumped into categories similar to downhill snow skiing today. One could choose from straight, gently sloped, novice type runs to others that were far more hair-raising and guaranteeing some loss of blood and possible broken bones. For boys, this decision is always a no-brainer. However, it was impossible to enjoy this activity for hours at a time because nosy neighbors and some motorists always reported us to the police out of unwarranted concerns for our safety and well-being. We scoffed at the suggestion that crashing into a moving vehicle could result in serious injury. On many occasions a police cruiser with lights flashing scattered boys like a bird dog scatters a covey of quail. This unnecessary intrusion forced us to adopt a more stealth-like approach to racing where we were able to get in a couple of runs and be long gone before the law arrived.   By carefully observing which neighbors were away from home and employing a gang of lookouts stationed at strategic places, we were able to continue to enjoy this activity until we grew older and moved on to bigger and better things.   Unfortunately, until this transition occurred, our neighbors continued to view us as a gang of ruffians and scoff-laws.

The area known as East Florence was a beehive of train activity during their heyday but it has lessened considerably over the years. Their proximity to our old home place made it impossible not to be aware of their constant presence because we could hear the whistles and rumbling as they moved through the area. There was a passenger station and a freight depot right in the middle of the community which had a noticeable effect on our daily movements. The main road was constantly being blocked as trains passed through headed toward other destinations or were being coupled together or separated in a small yard. From there the individual freight cars were diverted to the warehouses, knitting mills, coal yards and barrel stave factory nearby.   Anytime a train moved across a road, a man was stationed there with a brightly burning flare to warn traffic of the approaching train. The flare burned sort of like a giant sparkler. A new one looked like a stick of dynamite with a spike on the end to stick in the ground. These were treasures highly sought after by the boys living nearby. We darted in to claim them after the train had passed and the worker jumped on to the end of the last slowly moving freight car and moved on. These things burned at a temperature which rivaled the surface of the sun but we loved them. They were great to play with and could always be traded for something of greater value, like marbles or cigarettes. On the negative side, they were responsible for countless grass fires and several serious burns.

Frequently, the main body of the train would stop about a half mile north so that it would not block the main road. From there individual cars were uncoupled and allowed to roll down the very slight grade, powered only by gravity, to be shuttled to other sidings where they were to be loaded or unloaded as the situation dictated.   This provided a great opportunity for fun for boys without enough sense to appreciate the danger involved. We waited out of sight and as the box car moved slowly past we ran alongside and grabbed the ladder, using it to hoist ourselves aboard.   We had time to enjoy the ride for a few minutes before jumping off to avoid detection.

My Uncle Carlos was fond of telling this motley gang of boys there wasn't enough brains in the whole bunch to keep a jaybird from flying backwards. He was right!

Mountains and Mopeds

My very first trip to the Smoky Mountains came in 1980. Certainly I knew about the mountains but the opportunity, or the funds, never became available until this time. The trip was attractive to me because it was a place I had wanted to visit and, more importantly, all my expenses were paid. It was the annual meeting of state education association presidents, of which I had recently become a member. This august group met as frequently as possible in such touristy locales as Boston, Honolulu, San Juan, Seattle, San Diego and Miami. It is amazing how creative folks can be with other people's money whether it is taxes or membership dues, as long as it comes out of someone else's pocket.

The site selection committee, surprisingly, chose the little mountain town of Gatlinburg, Tennessee as a meeting place to fly in people from every state in the union as well as Puerto Rico and a couple of folks from Europe. This was probably their idea of roughing it and relating to the downtrodden people of Appalachia at the same time.

Normally, one would drive from northwest Alabama to Gatlinburg but transportation was a problem for me. Both my vehicles were prone to mechanical failure at any time. It was necessary for my wife to keep our semi-reliable car for work and to taxi our children to their everyday activities. My old pickup was not dependable enough to drive any distance without first contacting AAA to have a tow truck on stand-by for the inevitable breakdown. Consequently, I flew to Atlanta and then to Knoxville where I was met and driven to the meeting hotel in Gatlinburg. My means of transportation left me basically afoot whenever I needed to leave the hotel. There was no car for me to hop in and do any sightseeing. Our meeting covered most of a week and was held in, what was then, the Sheraton, overlooking the city from the top of a nearby mountain.

During breaks and between meetings I frequently walked down the mountain and explored the quaint little town of Gatlinburg. It was October so I visited the craft show at the civic center, rode to the top of a mountain on a ski lift, saw tons of chocolate being made on marble slabs and did my best to eat more than my fair share. One can explore most of the little town in a day and soon I had exhausted all the sights one could visit on foot. However, there was a little place near the civic center where one could rent a motorcycle. I had walked past the building several times without really noticing it before the idea began to take hold in my mind, why walk when I could ride? Besides, this would be my only chance to see the mountains from up close. I had visions of myself astride a big Harley rumbling through the town and into the mountains with the wind in my face and the gawking tourists in my wake. I would leave behind the glitter and plastic of a tourist town and see the mountains as God had created them. However, the situation was not exactly as advertised. Instead of renting Harleys, they were renting mopeds. For the uninitiated, a moped is a glorified bicycle. It is bulkier than a normal bike and is equipped with a small, gasoline engine and pedals. The fact that the contraption had pedals should have alerted me right off to a possible problem. We all know that foresight is never 20/20 as is hindsight. Another fatal oversight on my part was not noticing the size of what some engineer had obviously mistaken for an internal combustion engine. This motor could possibly have been intended for some kind of vehicle which was designed to move perpetually downhill with a stiff tail wind. Another design flaw was the brakes. The machine was designed to be stopped by applying pressure on handbrakes mounted on each handlebar. Apparently the design engineer felt whoever was riding would almost never want to actually apply the brakes and interfere with what little forward motion the engine could generate, so stopping was not a priority. Therefore, attaching real brakes to such a puny vehicle would be a waste of money.   More will be said about this almost fatal design defect later.

Again, a red flag should have been sent up, but I was ready for adventure, or so I thought. This entire episode turned out to be a case study in using something for which it was not intended. Canoes are not built to cross oceans, human beings are not designed to do push-ups and eat broccoli, kites are not designed to fly to the moon, and mopeds should not be driven in mountainous terrain, no matter what the manufacturer, or the pimply-faced teenager renting them to suckers like me, claims. Not being familiar with motorbikes of any kind, I was somewhat reluctant to take the plunge but the lure to view firsthand the beauty of the mountains soon overcame my caution. The young fellow at the rental place was very informative and assured me learning to drive the machine would not be a problem.

Have you ever noticed that many people who try to sell you something have no idea what they are talking about? The young lady at the building supply store always seems to be about sixteen years old and doesn't know a wing nut from posthole diggers. The guy selling lawn mowers lives in a condo and has never actually walked on grass but has seen it from the sidewalk. Be that as it may, he gave me some quick instructions, watched me drive across the parking lot for thirty seconds and pronounced me a qualified moped operator. For safety purposes, and to boost his commission, he rented me a helmet with a tinted visor. The contraception was so large that I could actually spin it around while it was on my head. It gave me a Darth Vader look and, more importantly, allowed me to remain anonymous in case any of my colleagues saw me or if the ride proved to be a fool's folly. If only I had known! Since my goal was to see majestic mountain vistas, I asked the rental guy where such could be viewed in the least amount of time as I needed to return to the hotel before the next meeting. He directed me to what is known as the Roaring Fork Motor Trail which began a short distance from where we stood. The trail is basically a one way trip over a nearby mountain, taking in fantastic views, old cabins, bubbling brooks, waterfalls and old growth forests. It is eleven miles in length and laid out in a loop which brought me back close to the downtown area without having to get on heavily traveled roads.   This was exactly what I wanted to see so I eased out of the parking lot and was on my way. Soon I was at the edge of town and civilization was in my rearview mirror, so to speak. Old cabins and barns came into view, certainly worth further exploration at a later date when I had more time.   Everything was fine as I putt-putted along on the moped. After a couple of miles of relatively flat land, the one way road began and started to ascend the side of the mountain. The little motor started to struggle but we were still making headway. The road continued to get steeper and steeper and the horsepower faded rapidly. It was soon apparent that I would have to use the pedals and assist the engine. Then I had my first revelation. Maybe that is why they put the pedals on in the first place!

It was hard to enjoy the view and pedal furiously at the same time so, it goes without saying, my trip ceased to be enjoyable and soon became a lot like work. The road got steeper, the motor grew weaker and I pedaled faster. The engine and I both gave out about the same time. Some obscure law of physics having to do with energy and forward motion, I must have missed that class in school, had undoubtedly been violated and I was at a standstill on the side of a very steep mountain with no top in sight. Then, just when one would think it couldn't get any worse, it did. The engine quit! Not knowing what awaited me, I decided to push the bike on to the top, since the road was one way and I still had hopes of completing my journey. This uncharacteristic optimism soon disappeared. My hopes rose as I rounded each switchback to have them fall when nothing but more switchbacks stretched as far as I could see. The top was not yet in sight. The optimism I spoke of earlier began to vanish at this point. Somehow, this wretched little machine had been transformed from a few pounds of metal with wheels to a large block of concrete and I was being forced to push it up a very steep mountain. However, as with life, a great deal of sweat and determination won over and the summit was eventually reached. The engine still wouldn't cooperate and refused to start as I furiously kicked down on the

The moped is not intended for use in a mountainous terrain.

starting pedal time after time. My efforts produced not even a sputter from the snuff-can size engine. Sweating, out of breath, in the throes of exhaustion, and thoroughly discouraged, I rolled the cursed bike over to the side of the road and pondered my fate. Dozens of cars passed with the occupants waving gaily as if they were in a parade. At least they didn't throw candy.   Foolish pride kept me from flagging someone down and begging for help but I didn't want the little children to see a grown man cry.   Finally, a Good Samaritan sensed my misery and pulled over. Another miracle occurred when I discovered the fellow actually knew something about small engines and was soon able to get it cranked.   After thanking him profusely, I jumped aboard the little bike and was again puttering across the crest of the mountain. The views were fantastic. My troubles were fading fast behind me on this glorious fall afternoon. Stretched out before me was mile after mile of mountain peaks and valleys, some obscured by the smoky haze from which the mountains derive their name. It could only be described as a visual feast, everything I had hoped to see. My Scottish Highlander heritage told me I had returned to my ancestral home. No sandy beaches of Florida for me. No skyscrapers, no honking traffic, no bustling mobs of people. I would return dozens of times over the next several years and still enjoy it to this day. But first, I had one other major task awaiting me. I had to go down the mountain. The level road across the crest of the mountain soon ended and the descent began. Had I only known, I would have gotten off and gone down the same way I came up, pushing the bike. As the downhill grade got steeper, I began to pick up speed at an alarming rate.   In spite of steady pressure on the handbrakes, they only slowed me down to something less than breakneck speed. The brakes were simply not able to stop the machine on the steep downhill descent. It could possibly have had something to do with the fact it was far exceeding the weight limit it was designed to carry.   As the road snaked and turned back on itself, the grade never leveled out so that I could stop and give my hands some relief. Mind you, they weren't just gentle left and right curves. They were engineered by some madman and seemed to loop around like a gigantic roller coaster. The muscles in my hands and forearms were becoming paralyzed from gripping the brakes. My hands were frozen into a claw like grip. If I tried easing up on one brake for relief the moped shot forward even faster. Downhill I sped, leaning into the curves and looking more and more like a motorcyclist in a competitive race. This was fast becoming far more of a challenge than I had in mind when I left the parking lot. My life flashed before my eyes and I realized no one knew where I was. The road clung to the side of the mountain on one side and was a sheer drop off on the other. If I went over the side I would never be found. Food for the bears! The trees had trunks the size of a Studebaker and were capable of stopping a runaway log truck. If I smacked into one of those things, I was a sure goner. They would have to remove me with an ice scraper. Would this road never end? As if the situation couldn't get any worse, it did. Horror of horrors, it had begun to rain! My visor was covered with water and I couldn't see but a few feet in front of me. When I turned loose of the brake to wipe the water away I picked up more speed. Wind was whistling through the helmet and roaring out the ear holes. I couldn't see or hear, as if hearing would make a difference. Rain water was running down my neck and I was soon drenched. The stench of the brake pads sizzling against the rubber tires burned my nose! Only the rain kept them from bursting into flames. What a nightmare! Up ahead, I spotted a SUV pulled over to enjoy the view. A couple and their little children were standing in the rain beside the road, which curved sharply in front of them. I felt like a pilot trying to steer a crippled plane away from a crowded city. Please Lord, don't let me hit one of them. They stood mesmerized by the sight of me rocketing toward them. Over the roar in my ears I could hear someone screaming. My only thought was why are these people screaming at me? Then I realized the screams were my own. I was screaming to warn them to run for their lives but they just smiled and waved. Only the strength one gets from sheer terror allowed me to wrestle the demented machine toward the middle of the road. I can only imagine what they were thinking. I wanted to smile and wave back and reassure them that I was not a threat, at least intentionally, but I couldn't turn loose of the brake. As I sped by, leaning into the curve and spewing gravel in all directions, I could hear the little girl say to her mother, "Mommy, look how fast that man is riding that bicycle." Little did they know they were probably observing a miracle, a dead man riding past them on a moped.

Finally, the descent slackened and the road began to level out and my ordeal came slowly to an end. I stopped the bike and placed both feet on the ground. I wanted to get off and kiss the good earth but I knew my trembling legs wouldn't support me. The return trip downtown was without incident. The rain had stopped and the sun broke through the clouds. I could again hear birds singing and the day returned to some semblance of normality. It was as if the last couple of hours had been nothing but a bad dream. While waiting at a traffic light in Gatlinburg, I glanced at my reflection in a store window. What a sight! I was wet, disheveled and the hot sun had caused my clothes to steam. The resemblance to a big, wet bear on a tricycle was scary. There was a lot I wanted to say to the young man at the rental place and he seemed eager to hear about my trip. I only told him it was a trip like no other I had ever taken and I had to hurry because I was late for a meeting.

Church Cat

One Sunday my wife and I had to stay after the evening worship service for a committee meeting. By the time we left, it was almost dark and the parking lot was virtually empty. Our house is located about ten miles from church and we were almost home when my wife thought she had heard a strange noise. We stopped, listened for a few moments and drove on after hearing nothing. However, as we turned into our carport, both of us heard a distinctive meowing sound coming from under the hood. There was no longer any doubt as to what we were hearing. We have a rather large dog and keeping a cat is not an option, for the cat's sake. Instead of raising the hood and having a frightened cat run into the woods and worsening the problem, I backed out and drove down to the end of the driveway. Sure enough, a cat about half grown was perched atop the motor. Trying to decide what to do, we concluded our only option was to go back to the church parking lot and turn the cat loose in hopes it would return home. To avoid being scratched by a strange cat, my wife wrapped it in a towel she kept in the back of the van. Off we went, back to the church in the dead of night. The cat was rather calm at first, but became increasingly agitated when it couldn't get away from my wife. It soon grew frantic and began to make a yowling sound cats make that is so irritating. My worst fear was realized when the creature managed to escape and ran across the dashboard to my side. All I needed was a cat blocking my vision. My wife snared it again and we sped through the darkness with the cat making terrible noises. The trip couldn't end soon enough for us or the cat.

As we pulled into the pitch black, deserted church parking lot, I cautioned my wife not to just drop the cat out the door. With nowhere else to hide, it would likely just run back under the car and climb onto the motor again. In hopes of avoiding this, she took the cat twenty to thirty feet away before turning it loose. It was too dark to tell what direction the cat ran when released so she hurriedly made her way back to the car. Apparently, twenty to thirty feet was not far enough because, unbeknownst to us at that moment, the frightened animal did seek shelter back under the car. This became apparent when we drove away and we felt the wheels bump as they crossed over the cat. Yes, we actually ran over the cat we were trying to help. Its limp body was visible from the glow of my brake lights and it was evident the cat did not survive our attempt to save it. This was a classic case of good intentions going haywire. We were too distraught to retrieve it that night so I returned to church early the next morning to take care of the situation. I was taken by surprise to find a sheriff's patrol car with two deputies inside parked very close to the dead cat. Were they waiting for the criminal to return to the scene of the crime? I decided they were either taking a break or waiting for some scoff law to run the stop sign at the corner and slap a ticket on him. However, they did seem somewhat surprised when I stopped and loaded the corpse into the back of my truck. I tried to act very nonchalant and look as if loading dead cats from the church parking lot into the back of my truck was the kind of activity that was part of my every day routine. Apparently they were not interested in me because they only looked on as I drove away. I took the dead cat back to our house and gave it a decent burial in our yard. We figured we owed it that much. However, this did not end our nightmare.

A few days later, we learned that our new pastor's cat was missing from the parsonage directly across from the church parking lot. Horrors, had I killed the pastor's cat? He and his wife had three little girls and had, only recently, moved to our church and probably brought the cat with them. They would surely think we were a bunch of barbarians for killing their cat. I had to come clean about what had happened so I waited for the opportune time to broach the subject. Actually, there is no opportune time to bring up an unsavory subject like the one I had on my mind, but it had to be done. I had no prior experience in tactfully explaining to a man of the cloth that I had killed his children's cat while trying to rescue it and this made it very difficult to get the confession underway. After hearing me out, while graciously holding back his laughter, he assured me that it was not his family's cat that had fallen victim to our clumsy rescue effort. Their cat was a different color and much larger and had already returned home. I may have totally misread the situation, but I got the impression he was not altogether sorry it was not his cat. Thank goodness, his little children didn't have to attend church with the awful man who had killed their little kitten. What a burden off my shoulders. But, at least, as my favorite comedian, the late Jerry Clower, was fond of saying, "We gave it a sporting chance."

Pa Mac

There are so many males in the McDonald family with the given name, "William," they are hard to keep separate. My grandfather was Jesse William, my father was William Ervin, my oldest brother was William Lindsey, our son is William Thomas and his son is William Grant. Our son is called "Will" by those who know him and we are extremely proud that he and his wife allowed the name "William" to touch five generations of our family by giving their youngest son that name.

My grandfather, Jesse William, was called by a variety of names. His friends called him "Will Mac" and I often heard others refer to him as "Old Man Will." His grandchildren simply called him, "Pa." He was born in 1878, the fifth of ten children of his father, John Scruggs McDonald. My oldest brother, William L. McDonald, has thoroughly researched and written volumes about our family before and after our grandfather and there is no need for me to repeat any of his work, which is far superior to anything I could ever produce. As I have grown older, many of my thoughts seem to return to events of my childhood. Both my grandfathers were well along in years when I was a boy but I do have many memories of both but didn't know either of them well. Both passed away when I was very young but I was twelve when my grandfather McDonald died.

Pa Mac was a big part of our life because he lived with us from long before I was born until his last few years. Unfortunately, those years were spent in Bryce Hospital until his death in 1957. Older Alabamians will immediately recognize Bryce as "the insane asylum," as it was called for many years. Bryce Hospital is located in Tuscaloosa and was the home for thousands of people, designated as mentally ill by some authority in their home town, until the state decided to phase it out and gradually replace it with a newer facility to be located in the same city. The old Bryce property is adjacent to the University of Alabama campus and its old buildings are a landmark for many people. Bryce opened in 1861 as the Alabama Insane Hospital and in its

The author and his grandfather, Jesse William McDonald.

declining years the conditions inside could only be described as deplorable, at best.   It is not my intent to continue to criticize the institution as that would be akin to throwing rocks at a man already on his way to the gallows.

It has always saddened me that I never got to know this man as most boys would like to remember their grandfather.   There were no fishing trips to the nearby creek, no tossing the baseball in the front yard, no

Grandfather, Jesse William and some of his grandsons. Front, left to right, Tom, not happy and John. Rear left to right, Joe, Bob, Pa Mac and Bill.

stories about the adventures he had experienced in his life, and no advice on how to live my life.   Instead, I knew him only as the grouchy old man who occupied a room in our house and a seat at our table and who was probably the cause of many bitter arguments between my parents.   Recently, I began seeking out the opinions of surviving siblings and cousins and all of them felt pretty much the same way, he was a grumpy, ill-tempered man in his old age and, unfortunately, that was the only time of his life I knew him.   There is no doubt that I could have been a much better grandson and maybe have made his life more pleasant had I not been so naïve.

I remember my grandfather was always dressed in a black wool suit, with a black vest and hat and always wore a white shirt.   Blue eyes have run in the male members of our family for generations and his were the brightest blue I have ever seen. Virtually everyone who knew my grandfather remarked on his blue eyes. He was a carpenter by trade and worked at the Florence Wagon Works helping build the wagons which were touted to be among the best in the country. His wife, Lillie, died when my father was only about five years old and he never remarried.   Pa came to live with my parents during the

Great Depression after our family's house was taken by creditors when Daddy lost his job. This catastrophic time forced Daddy to move his family into two tents for several years. One tent was for sleeping and the other for cooking. My brother Joe remembers when Daddy petitioned off the rear part of the kitchen tent for our grandfather to call his home. He responded in the following way to my request for his memories of our grandfather:

"When I was about three or four years old, I remember living in two tents behind Daddy's aunt, Lott Lindsey's, house. I can remember Mother, Daddy, Bill and me slept in the tent that had a wood floor. The other tent was used as a kitchen with sawdust floor and part of it was closed off as Pa had his bed in behind the stove and table. Pa Mac did the same as he always did as best as I can remember. He would leave in the morning and be back home at 11:30 a.m. for dinner. He then went back to Sweetwater and back home around 5:00p.m., for supper. We used to go out to what was called the "wood yard", where K-Mart used to be. All that was woods back then and that was where we got wood for the stove. Aunt Lott's husband had a mule and wagon and Daddy would get it to go get the wood. Pa always went and helped cut and bring the wood home. At that time Daddy did not work nor did most people who lived in East Florence.

From there we moved across the ditch into a four room house that belonged to a Mr. Pounders, who also lived on Sweetwater Avenue. Somebody that Daddy knew had a bus (like a school bus). He gave Daddy a job driving the bus every day from in front of the Florence Courthouse to Phil Campbell, Alabama, and back every day of the week. I don't remember too much about that but I do remember when we moved up to the house on Staunton Avenue. It was a four room house but Daddy and Pa got enough lumber to build a room on the back for Pa. Later on, after Daddy went to work, he bought lumber to build the kitchen on the back. I remember Pa had a half bed in the small room that they first built for him. Maybe it was a half bed and a chifferobe (a piece of furniture with drawers, a small closet and mirror).

I never knew Pa to take a bath at home, even after Daddy put in a bath tub. Nick, at Nick's Barber Shop in East Florence, had a shower in the back room that you could take a shower for 25 cents, with towel included. One day while I was getting a haircut, before I went into the Navy, he asked me was Pa sick? I told him not that I know of. He said Pa usually came in on Wednesday to take a shower. I told him I didn't know that. I had always wondered, as I knew he did not take a bath at home. He said Mr. Mac had been taking showers there for several years once every two weeks, sometimes every week.

Pa smoked a pipe and used snuff. He had false teeth and when he would get up from eating he would go over to the sink, take out his teeth and wash them and put them back in his mouth. Mother would change his sheets once a week, if she washed that week, depending on the weather. Before she got a washer, she had to boil water out back in a black kettle with two #two wash tubs, then wring them out and hang them out to dry, winter or summer. Pa would never give her a thank you or offer her any money. I guess she always washed his clothes and made his bed. Pa was not a very friendly man and very seldom did I ever see him laugh. He had a girlfriend on Cherry Hill and one over by Ashcraft Cotton Mill. I know this because he would ask me to take him to see one of them. He also had a woman who lived on the road toward town.

I never knew much about Pa, except after I got out of the Navy he would always ask me to take him to Mississippi to see his cousin who lived outside of Corinth. He would get mad if I told him I didn't have time, or had something I had to do. After I got out of the Navy the first time, January 1950, I bought a 1937 Chevrolet with a floor shift for $200.00. He always wanted to borrow it to go to Mississippi or he would ask me to take him. I told him I didn't believe he knew how to drive a car. He said that he did. So, one evening after I got off from work I went by to see Mother and Daddy. Pa was on the front porch before I could get out of the car. I always parked in the front yard. He came over and said he wanted to show me he could drive. I gave in and he got in on the driver's side and I got in on the other side. I said, "Pa, can you go up the hill without hitting the tree?" He said he could. He didn't hit the tree but he almost scraped it doing about 25-30 mph. He started down the big hill and I told him to slow down. Finally I had to put my foot over on the brake to stop the car. He got mad and got out of the car and didn't talk to me for a week. Pa was a stubborn and a high tempered man. It was his way or nothing at all. Shortly after that I reenlisted back into the Navy and never really saw him much until he died in 1957, a couple of years after I went back into the Navy...........If you went through Sweetwater any time of the day, except at dinner, you would see him sitting on one of the benches at one of the stores. Back then, all stores had a bench out front and a top over the front so if it rained they would keep dry. But even if it rained or snowed, he would go to East Florence and maybe to town. He had a routine and I never knew him to ever miss going on his daily mission.

This is about all I can remember about Pa. I just knew he was stubborn, high tempered, wore black and never would speak unless you spoke first. After I went in the Navy I never forgot him and I think of some of the things he would do. He didn't like too many people. One was Poppa Lindsey (our other grandfather) and another was Mr. Lester Staggs, or any Staggs as he used to go with their mother and people thought they would get married. Our cousin, Charles McDonald, may know a little about him as on Sundays he would go to their house for breakfast if Mother didn't get up early enough to fix his breakfast at home."

My older brothers remember Pa when he was a much younger man and their memories are far different from mine. They knew him before living in the midst of seven grandchildren and old age wore him down. One sort of peculiar memory I have of my grandfather is his absolute refusal to eat what he called "light bread," or the white store bought loaf bread of today. He either ate corn bread or no bread. Pa Mac vowed it would kill you and, in hindsight, he may have been right, according to those who have studied all the harmful effects of the ingredients of "light bread". My other grandfather, Leonard Lindsey, had moved his grocery store from downtown Sweetwater to the front room of his home on the same street on which we lived. My Grandfather McDonald would sit on our front porch and shout his dire predictions to anyone passing our house with a loaf of bread in their hand. Many of our neighbors paid my Grandfather Lindsey an extra penny for a paper sack in which to hide their bread purchase simply to escape the wrath of Pa Mac. He left our house at exactly the same time every morning and walked to East Florence. He sat on the benches there and spent the morning with his friends before walking back to our house for lunch. After lunch, he repeated the routine and returned home in time for supper. His daily walk was predictable to those along his route and many could tell the time of day by waiting for him to pass by on his walk. He carried a huge gold, conductor type watch in a vest pocket with a gold chain looping down out of the pocket. He carried a plug of Red Man chewing tobacco in his vest pocket and during most of his waking hours he had a chew in his mouth.

The fact that my grandfather died in an insane asylum has been a source of embarrassment for me most of my life, especially when I was young. While I have never discussed these feelings with any of my siblings or cousins, I suspect some of them harbored the same type thoughts. In later years my embarrassment has turned to disgust over the way our society has historically treated those diagnosed with mental illness. Maybe this policy could best be described as "out of sight, out of mind." While I was in school at the University of Alabama, my wife and I lived in married student housing only a short distance away from the place he died. I never passed the old buildings without thinking of my grandfather and how miserable his last few years must have been as a patient in that institution. It is ironic that while researching a project for a graduate class at the university I spent some time in the building in which he died. Daddy told me once about how the county sheriff's deputies transported my grandfather to Tuscaloosa handcuffed in the back seat of their patrol car because he had been combative during his short stay in a local nursing home. I visited him only one time while he was living at the mental hospital. My daddy and his brother, my Uncle Alphonse, were going on a visit and they allowed me and my brothers Johnny and Bill to go with them, with Bill being the driver. We were passed through locked doors down a long, gloomy hall to a dark room where my grandfather lay on a narrow bed. After just a few minutes in the room I stood outside in the hall where it was not so scary. Whether he was aware of our visit or not, I do not know.   He mercifully passed away a short time later. His funeral, at the Freewill Baptist Church on Sweetwater Avenue, was the first I had ever attended. My questions about the time he spent there have been legion and unanswered because they were asked only in my mind.   This was a topic about which there was very little discussion. The most important question I have always really wondered about could only be answered by my grandfather. Did he know where he was and did he feel abandoned? Maybe it is wishful thinking on my part to even wonder if he felt abandoned.

A short time after the death of my grandfather, something happened in a house atop the hill where we lived that brought back memories of Bryce Hospital. Long before I was born, the teenage daughter of a couple across the street from us just disappeared, with no explanation to any of the neighbors.   It was rumored she had been confined to Bryce Hospital for all those years but her parents never spoke to anyone about the specifics of the situation, only saying it was a family matter. Then, as suddenly as she disappeared, she reappeared at their house. Of course, I did not know the young girl that left our hill but an old lady, at least in my eyes, returned in her place. She had been gone, some estimated, about fifty years.   For as long as we continued to live across the street, I never saw her leave the swing on their front porch.

There is a lot of sadness associated with a place like Bryce. The cemetery I passed hundreds of times while living and attending school nearby was all the proof I needed. Many patients died in the institution with no family to claim their remains or, maybe, families that refused to even acknowledge their kinship.   These poor souls were buried on a hillside on the back of the property that was intentionally out of sight for many, many years. However, as the city and university grew, new roads were built and one of the major new entrances to the expanded campus passed within a few feet of this sad place where abandoned people were buried and long forgotten. Perhaps it is only fitting that their final resting place is now in the public eye lest we forget that society, as a whole is capable of mistakes, just as are individuals.

Milking

There is evidence that mankind has used milk as a food source farther back than history could ever be recorded. Etchings and paintings inside caves inhabited by man since the dawn of civilization show what appear to be people and cows in close proximity. While milk from cows seems to be preferred by most folks in this country, other societies might prefer camel milk or reindeer milk or maybe even goat milk. There are those who may even remember a time when milk was delivered door to door by someone called, you won't believe this, the milkman. As for me, milk is the nectar of life. Give me a quart of milk and some donuts or cookies and a good book to read and I'll be as content as a cow chewing her cud, so to speak. Sometimes on the news they will have segments showing how schools are trying to teach children where their food comes from, especially milk. They visit farms and watch someone milking a real cow by hand instead of conveniently finding milk in a container purchased at the local grocery store, or in a tiny carton at school. This is good information to have but it is a shame it has to be taught in school, especially when the time could be used more productively teaching reading, writing and arithmetic and trying to catch up with the Chinese. When I was growing up, even the dumbest among us knew the source of their milk. There were cows and goats everywhere and some of us even had to milk the critters.

My oldest brother, Bill, taught me the fine art of milking a cow. It took a while before he felt I could handle all that responsibility. It was a great day when I was turned loose to do it all on

This milking stool was made by W. E. McDonald in the mid 1950's and used by his sons.

my own. Bill got up early and milked before leaving for work. My job was to milk every evening and then put the cow in the barn so my brother wouldn't have to round her up the next morning. Rounding up a cow accustomed to being milked is not normally a difficult job. As a matter of fact, most times the cow will meet you at the barn at milking time just for the relief of unloading a bag full of milk and to receive a big helping of molasses rich feed that smelled sweet enough for kids to eat, which, I must admit, was a great temptation. My daddy used to say in describing having to go to work every day, "The work ain't hard and the time ain't long, but it sure is regular." The same is true of milking a cow. It has to be done every day or the cow will dry up. It is a seven day a week chore. There is no vacation time for someone with the responsibility of having cows to milk. The only respite is when the cow decides it is time to wean the calf and she dries up until she gives birth to the next calf. No wonder all the dairy farmers are selling out and their land going to developers.

Milking a cow is more than just grabbing a teat and watching the milk flow. It takes warm hands and strong fingers to be successful in coaxing the milk into the pail. However, a great deal of the process depends upon a cooperative cow. If there is a calf at hand, some cows may hold back the milk and save it for the calf. This requires some trickery and sleight of hand on the part of the one milking the cow. The cow can be tricked by allowing the calf to nurse for a few seconds and then put the calf back into the stall. By then the udder is full again and milking can continue. Of course, the larger the calf the harder it is to get it away from the cow. Some cows will kick you if they become annoyed or agitated and vigilance is always necessary when milking a kicking cow. The old jersey I first milked was a kicker and she landed quite a few blows before I finally figured out where to place my stool to avoid her back leg. An inch was as good as a mile as long as she missed.

Fresh cow's milk that has not been subjected to additives or homogenized is a delicacy that is fast disappearing from our tables in this country. It is an acquired taste and most folks today would probably turn it down. We stored our milk in one gallon, glass, wide mouth jars. After the jars sat in the refrigerator for a little while, the cream would rise to the top and form a thick layer covering the milk. Drinking that crème with my cold glass of milk was a pleasure my taste buds will never forget. People came from all over to buy those gallon jugs of milk with the cream showing at the top. We kept a spare refrigerator on the back porch with a can nearby in which they deposited their money. We sold it for fifty cents a gallon as long as they left their empty jug and it was all done on the honor system if we weren't at home. Today, one would have to spend time in jail for selling milk that had not been pasteurized or homogenized.

Fortunately, those good times of having plenty of fresh milk were revisited after my wife and I married and had children. Three milk drinkers in a family of four consume a lot of milk and I, being my father's son, figured money could be saved by milking my own cows. As a matter of fact, my daddy made me a three legged milking stool which I used and is still in my possession after all these years. My first purchase was an old brindle cow that would nurse anything from her own calf to an elephant, she didn't seem to care. I bought orphan calves at the sale barn for just a few dollars and she would nurse them to weaning size. After a while, I added a younger jersey which doubled the size of my herd. Fortunately, our neighbor just across the fence had a bull that liked to come and visit when the time was right. It was a no-brainer when deciding whether to buy my own bull or just patch the fence after he had visited for a couple of weeks. A fence is not much of a deterrent to a bull with romance on his mind. Since I had to feed the bull only a few days a year and my neighbor was relieved of that responsibility for those same few days and I wound up with two new calves every year, everything turned out all right for me, my neighbor, the bull and the cows. My only cost was a locust post and a few staples.

My daily routine was to get up before dawn and go to the barn to milk both cows before getting ready and leaving for work. My barn did not have the benefit of electric lights so I carried a kerosene lantern which gave out as much light as a paper match. The cows were already in the barn, having been with their calves all day and separated at night so the calves would not drink up all the milk. Milking in the winter was not fun at all because it was always very dark and, most of the time, very cold and the cow would not appreciate the use of work gloves. The process became so familiar that many mornings I milked both cows without ever seeing them. It was so dark in the barn and my light so poor, I had to feel my way around. The old brindle cow was a joy to milk. She gave it all she had and never tried to leave before the job was completed. Her colleague was not so cooperative. Being young, she was hard to keep in one place and was prone to kick. She did give a lot of creamy, tasty milk but you had to work hard for it. When I decided to downsize, she was the one to go.

One has to be cautious when drinking fresh, non- pasteurized milk. To prevent any chance of milk borne diseases, I took both my cows to the vet every year for shots and blood work. There are many experiences one can have while driving that produce stress and butterflies in the stomach, to put it mildly. My old truck was not large enough or strong enough to haul both cows at the same time so I had to make two trips. Loading a half ton cow in the back of a short wheel base, half ton pickup with low wooden side boards and driving thirty miles round trip to the vet is a harrowing experience at best and nauseating at worst. If the cow would only stand perfectly still in the middle of the truck bed, it would be an almost tolerable experience. However, for some reason, the cow tends to walk around or stand predominantly on one side of the bed which causes considerable list, sort of like a ship about to tip over on its side. There is a constant fear the cow will simply tumble out of the truck over the side boards, or the truck will tip over. If either occurs, your day will take a sudden turn for the worst.

Since we had volumes of milk and couldn't possibly drink it all, it was only logical that we churn our own butter. This process requires some patience and a good deal of repetitive labor. The sweet milk is poured into the churn, covered with a cloth and allowed to sit and begin to clabber, or turn sour. It is at that point that patience is no longer necessary and the labor part begins. The top of the churn is fitted with a wooden cover with a round hole in the middle. That hole is for the handle of the paddle to pass through. The person doing the churning sits and plunges the paddle in and out of the clabbered milk for hours at a time. This action causes the butter to separate from the milk and rise to the top. At the appropriate time, the butter is spooned off and placed in a butter mold to shape it. The remainder of the liquid in the churn is buttermilk which is quite tasty to many folks, including myself. If the term, "handmade" is an apt description of anything, it is of the butter making process.

As long as the cows stayed out of the bitter weed, drinking fresh milk was worth the effort involved. As with many good things in life, they eventually come to a close. Our job responsibilities increase and the kids begin to take part in activities outside of home and soon we find other things are occupying more and more of our time. Other, more comfortable, less demanding ways of doing things become the norm and another piece of the old way of life bites the dust. It is wrong headed to think old ways of doing things are always better than new ways, which they obviously are not. Those cold, dark mornings milking in the barn seem to have taken place in another life. Maybe that is where they belong.

Paperboy

Today, my daily newspaper is delivered by automobile by a person known as a paper carrier. My paper carrier has never been to my house and we have never spoken to each other. There seems to be such a high rate of turnover I would not recognize the carrier if we were to meet on the street. Each month we receive, from the business office, a bill for that month's deliveries and the payment is submitted directly to the company without ever being touched by the carrier. That is the nature of the world we live in today. This system has changed drastically from the time my brother and I delivered papers. We were paperboys, plain and simple, no sexist language intended. During the 1950's, my brother, Johnny, and I shared a paper route. At that time, it was an afternoon paper with Sunday being the only day of the week they printed a morning edition. The discipline of this responsibility served me well as I grew older and became involved in activities in which discipline was important. We had to hurry home from school every day, change clothes and then rush down to the front of our grandfather's store a few blocks away to pick up our bundle of papers when they were tossed from the delivery truck. Each of us carried a canvas bag with a shoulder strap to hold the day's deliveries. If it was wet or raining, we had to roll each paper and insert it in a clear plastic sack to keep it dry. On other days, we rolled the papers and placed a rubber band around the center to hold it together. This made it more convenient to toss onto the porch of our customer's house. Johnny and I had about one hundred customers, give or take a few each week, and we split it right down the middle with about fifty each.

Extra papers were thrown out a lot of days for us to sell on the street. We soon learned to stand in front of the knitting mill when they got off work at four o'clock and generally sold them all very quickly for a nickel each. This meant a few extra cents for us. Our regular route was entirely in a lower working class community where most had suffered through a lot of hard knocks in life and having a newspaper delivered to their house every day was one of the few luxuries they allowed themselves to enjoy. My half of the route took me up Sweetwater Avenue with a left turn up through what had always been known as "Railroad Hollow" and into a public housing project called Cherry Hill Homes. Johnny continued on up Sweetwater until a left turn carried him across several blocks until he reached the housing project. We went up the middle to the north side of the project with Johnny making all the deliveries on the right side and the left side belonged to me. We generally finished about the same time and walked back home together. At that time, the price for a weekday paper was five cents and fifteen cents for the Sunday edition. The paper company received three cents out of each weekday paper and ten cents on Sunday. This left us with two cents and five cents respectively. If everything went well, and it rarely did, we split from sixteen to eighteen dollars per week evenly. However, the hazards of being a paperboy were many. The weather was always our first hurdle for the paper had to be delivered regardless. Next, we had to do all the collecting ourselves. There was no office to receive the money and dispense it back to us. We collected every Friday and the weekly amount owed would be forty-five cents if they wanted a paper every day. We had to knock on every door and tell the customer we

were there to collect, as if they didn't already know. Most were cordial and collecting was no problem. However, collecting from some almost required holding them at gunpoint. It was not unusual for some customers, knowing they were about to move, went several weeks without paying and then skipped town. This was a big deal because we had to make up out of our own pocket what they owed when they moved. This potentially was a major loss to us each week. It was simply money down the drain and we never had the opportunity to recoup our losses because we never saw them again. Anybody who would intentionally stiff a twelve year kid is operating below the lowest rung on the ladder of society.

The man who literally struck terror into the heart of every paperboy was named Mr. Hunter Allen. His official title was Circulation Manager but to us he may as well have been the ogre living under the bridge in fairy tales. He came

Tommy, left and Johnny McDonald during their paperboy years.

43

to our house every Monday to pick up the money from the previous week's collection. He knew exactly how many papers had been dropped off for us and exactly how much money we owed the company. It didn't matter whether we had been paid for the papers or not, we had to pay him. He sat at our kitchen table while counting out every coin and bill. There was no such thing as telling him we will pay you next week. He operated strictly on a cash and carry basis. If our federal government counted pennies as diligently as Mr. Allen, there would never be a deficit.   In addition to causing stress among his young employees, Mr. Allen was always on the prowl trying to recruit new paperboys. Apparently the turnover rate was quite high in our profession. Maybe it had something to do with the fact we worked seven days a week in all kind of weather with no off days. My cousin Mike happened to be at our house one day Mr. Allen was there counting our money. Now, Mike was my very best friend in addition to being my cousin.   We were the same age so we had grown up together just a few houses apart. Although he was my best friend, in later years looking back on our many years together, I came to the conclusion he was not real perceptive or dependable, for that matter.   But he was shrewd enough to know he was not interested in a job and especially one working as a paperboy for Mr. Hunter Allen.   Mike frequently kept me company on my route and was familiar with the pitfalls of the job. But Mr. Allen had already sized him up and made a direct offer of immediate employment. Mike was somewhat backward and not accustomed to speaking directly to adults, especially concerning job offers. On his way out the door, Mike said something to the effect, "I ain't had no sperence," meaning of course he did not have any experience in that particular field of employment and did not consider himself qualified and, consequently, could not accept Mr. Hunter's offer of employment.   My brother and I used that phrase, "I ain't had no sperence" from that moment on as sort of a private joke between us when faced with something we were not interested in doing.   Also, Mike studiously avoided our house anytime Mr. Allen's car was parked out front.

The customers of a paperboy back then were not nameless people we never saw or spoke to and lived in houses we never set foot in. We spoke to virtually every customer on our route almost on a daily basis. When the weather was bad, they often invited us into their homes on collection day. We stood beside their wood stove or fireplace while they opened their cloth coin purse and counted out the pennies, nickels and dimes with which to pay us. Today this would be throwaway change for most folks but to them every penny meant hard work at the mill or stove factory. They worked under conditions which would be banned by the government today, breathing saw dust and cotton fibers that would eventually clog their lungs and bring about a slow, painful death. They asked about us, how we were doing in school, who our parents were and what our daddy did for a living. Invariably, they knew one of our parents or grandparents. It was not unusual at all for them to give us a gift for Christmas, the most common being a box of chocolate covered cherries. With few exceptions, they were decent, hardworking people who worked hard for what little they had and would not accept charity. Many lived in what had once been mill houses and sat on their front porch when they could and talked to neighbors for entertainment. A television was extremely rare, the only air conditioner was a Sears fan in the window, a few had radios, almost none of them had a car, and some still had a privy somewhere out behind the house even though they may have recently installed running water and an indoor toilet.

Being a paperboy was not a major turning point in my life. Few of us experience events of a magnitude which actually changes our lives. However, my job as a paperboy taught me a lot about responsibility, the value of money, discipline and meeting and dealing with adults who were mostly friendly but with a few con artists sprinkled in. This was just one small piece of the picture that constitutes one's life. To me, life is the sum of all these little parts with each part building on the others. When it is all over we are defined as a person by the sum total of all those daily events. The most valuable thing I carried away from my job as a paperboy was all the time I was able to spend with my brother over those years. Neither of us knew it at the time but we were fast approaching the fork in the road of our lives Robert Frost spoke of in his poem "The Road Not Taken:"

Two roads diverged in a yellow wood
And sorry I could not travel both
And be one traveler, long I stood
And looked down one as far as I could
To where it bent in the undergrowth:
Then took the other, as just as fair,
And having perhaps the better claim,
Because it was grassy and wanted wear;
Though as for that the passing there
Had worn them really about the same,
And both that morning equally lay
In leaves no step had trodden black.
Oh, I kept the first for another day!
Yet knowing how way leads on to way,
I doubted if I should ever come back.
I shall be telling this with a sigh
Somewhere ages and ages hence:
Two roads diverged in a wood, and I-

45

I took the one less traveled by
And that has made all the difference.

   In a way we were both just bidding time until our boyhood expired and that time for Johnny was just around the corner.   Mine had a few more years on the meter but it was gaining a head of steam.   Usually, at that time of our life, we are blissfully unaware of what lies ahead. My brother was soon at the age when his cronies, fast cars and girls were much more important than hanging out with a little brother. My interests were still with bikes and horses and baseball. In a few short years he was far away in the military and I was in college and we were both miles down those diverging paths we had each taken with neither of us taking any time to think about a paper route.   But the best part of this story is that these roads that had diverged earlier soon began to merge back together and become one. We were to become close friends again and those years were some of the best times of my life.

Brandon School Memories

It's finally official. The old school building that is remembered so well from my boyhood has been long gone for many years.   Until now, however, the building that was once the newest version of Brandon School remained, even though it no longer functioned as a school. Now the decision has been made to construct a huge regional hospital on the old school site that will cover much of the surrounding neighborhood and it will forever vanish, covered by new buildings and an asphalt parking lot.   The regional hospital is much needed and will bring in new business, which will be good for the community. However, much of the working class neighborhood which characterized that part of town will be gone forever.   Brandon School has been the source of my family's elementary school years for several generations, and, for many, the only formal education they were ever privileged to acquire. The sons and daughters of generations of mill hands, store clerks, tradesmen, foundry, warehouse, and factory workers, and a whole host of ne'er-do-wells made up the vast majority of the thousands of pupils who walked those halls. I grew up not knowing a son or daughter of what most would call a professional person. In college, I learned we were all members of the lower working class. Fortunately, we did not know the difference. My grandparents, parents, siblings, cousins, aunts and uncles and nieces and nephews all made the daily trek up that old hill to sit and have some "book learning" drilled into our hard heads. Many of the same teachers taught two generations of my family and, bless their old hearts, deserved all the retirement benefits this miserly state doled out to them.

My first encounter with Brandon occurred when my next oldest brother, Johnny, did as he was told and took me to school on my first day and left me crying at the front steps. Despite this rather dismal beginning, my outlook on schooling improved considerably and I left six years later with nothing but good memories of the time spent behind those walls. The building that was so intimidating to me then was the handsome, red brick building that faced Ironside Street. It was fronted by a low rock wall that gradually grew taller as it followed the street downhill.   The building had a round, stone drinking fountain and flagpole to the left of the front sidewalk and window wells at intervals to provide sunlight to the rooms in the basement. The old white, wood-framed building it was supposed to replace was still standing behind this newer building and was used for as long as I was a student.

The newest version of the school is the round, modernistic monstrosity that will be demolished to make room for the new hospital. This building was erected long after I left and, believe it or not, had no walls between the classroom areas. It was supposed to be the greatest innovation in school construction of its time but the effectiveness of the "no walls" idea

SCHOOL DAYS 1953-54
BRANDON

The author's second grade picture from Mrs. Smyrl's room at Brandon.

48

was debated during its entire existence.

Structurally, the building of my boyhood was probably identical to many others built at that time using mass-produced blueprints. All the rooms had huge, high windows designed to catch any available breeze because air conditioning was far in the future for public schools in the South. Strangely enough, it had separate entrances for girls and boys, each identified by the appropriate gender engraved in a stone arch over the door. For some reason, they trusted us to sit next to each other in the classrooms, but not to come into the building together. The hall floors on the top floor were wood and freshly oiled each summer to soak up the dirt. The basement floors were concrete with two stairways connecting the two floors. To the left of the main front entrance was the principal's office, occupied by Mr. William Graham for the first five years of my stay at Brandon. He was a thin, scholarly fellow who was called, behind his back of course, "Ichabod" after the character in the book,

The author, after receiving his diploma during graduation ceremony at Brandon School in 1958.

Legend of Sleepy Hollow. An order to appear in his office was a virtual death knell, at least in their mind, to any student unfortunate enough to receive such a summons. Every kid in school knew Mr. Graham had an electric paddle secreted away in that dark place that could turn one's rear end into a huge blister. For some reason, we all believed Mr. Graham to be allergic to a popular wildflower called goldenrod. What value this bit of information had to our daily existence was never made clear but it was passed on to each generation of students, apparently hoping someone could make good use of that little tidbit of knowledge. I was to learn much later that this man was actually well respected in his profession and did many things, frequently paying out of his own pocket, for the, mostly very poor, children in his care.

Before I entered the sixth grade, a change took place in this office and Mr. Leo Creel became principal. When I later became a teacher in the Florence School system, Mr.

Creel and I became good friends and we often reminisced about Brandon School and the role it played in the lives of the people who lived in that part of the city.

Just a few feet from the main office, the halls split left and right, and made a complete loop around the school auditorium. It was in this seemingly cavernous room we had school assemblies and graduation. There aren't many school-wide assemblies these days, probably because the students don't know how to behave and administrators want to keep large gatherings to a minimum. Not so at Brandon! We had assemblies of some kind every week and loved it. School plays, yo-yo demonstrations, spelling bees, sing-alongs and authentic Native Americans showing us how to war dance caused us to eagerly flock to the auditorium. We were lined up and marched to our designated seats like soldiers in a parade. Sometimes it was even better than going to the movie and it didn't cost us a dime.   One of the biggest differences between kids of the 1950's and the kids of today may be that we knew how to appreciate the little things in life.

For the first five years I attended Brandon, we had no school cafeteria. Every day around lunch time, a covered truck appeared and huge pots of food were off loaded into the building. The pots were then placed on rolling, wooden carts and wheeled to each room by matronly women who accompanied the truck.   When the cart arrived at our door, we lined up and accepted the tray of food handed us by the cart ladies.   We ate at our desks and the used trays were later collected and went with the pots back to their mysterious point of origin, only to return day after day after day. We were not simply encouraged to eat everything on our tray, we were ordered to eat it. In those days teachers could do things like that. Evidently, all the teachers were reading from the same talking points because they were constantly pointing out to us the fact that there were millions of starving children in India and Africa.   However, what relationship that might have had with the boiled cabbage and macaroni on our plates was not forthcoming. Maybe the starving children would feel better if they knew we were eating food we considered disgusting. Since we were forbidden to return any uneaten food, a lot of it ended up stuffed into our desks. At the end of the day, we simply pulled it out and crammed it into our pants pocket. On the walk home we dumped it or fed it to dogs we happened to encounter.   My mother inquired on more than one occasion as to why there were bits of what appeared to be macaroni in my pants pocket?   Since all the girls wore dresses at that time, I was never clear how they handled their food disposal problem.

The very first school cafeteria opened at Brandon when I was in the sixth grade. We were as proud of that cafeteria as some people would be of a five-star restaurant. Sixth graders consider themselves to be the top dogs of an elementary school, kind of like seniors in a high school.   One day Mr. Creel came to our room and asked for some boys to move boxes into the new lunchroom. Eager to prove my emerging manhood, I volunteered without realizing the boxes to be moved weighed fifty pounds each. I was a skinny, scrawny kid and barely weighed ninety pounds. Mr. Creel seemed to get a big kick out of watching me shove, not lift, those boxes across the floor. Even as a sixth grader, I learned to be cautious about volunteering.

However, there were some good size boys in the upper elementary grades in those days that would have had no problem with moving heavy boxes. Once we completed the sixth grade at Brandon, we had to move to the big downtown junior high school. It was not only the size of the new school that intimidated us but it was an accepted fact of life that East Florence was considered by many to be on the wrong side of the tracks and we knew the kids from the other feeder schools knew it as well. It was not unusual for someone, mostly boys, to intentionally fail several grades so they would turn sixteen in the sixth grade and then be allowed to quit. Quitting school as soon as possible was a generations old tradition in many families, as it was in mine. They were determined not to have to make the change to a new school and it was more comfortable to just stay at Brandon and then quit. It wasn't real difficult back then for a sixteen year old to find a job at one of the knitting mills, warehouses or find some other type of unskilled labor in the community. Another option was to join the military at age seventeen, as did several of my brothers. A friend of mine named Jack actually drove a car to school in the fifth grade and parked it about a block away. He was just biding time until his sixteenth birthday.

Schools in those days were not hindered by due process rights for students and all the paperwork which went along with parental notification and permission to administer medical treatment was not yet part of the process. We were regularly lined up and given shots by nurses with absolutely no warning. Of course, any advance notification would have given us ample reason to be sick on the appointed day and not show up at school. As far as I can remember, refusal to take the shot was not an option. We were also checked regularly for lice and ringworm. Any kid who showed up wearing a toboggan and insisted on not removing it from his head was proof he had failed a ringworm check. The accepted remedy was to have his head shaved and painted with a purple medicine before he could return to school. All his friends ridiculed him unmercifully for a while but we all knew deep inside that for the grace of God, it could have been us.

There was one health issue of our young lives that was one of the most serious of my generation. Polio was the scourge of young children in the 1950's. At that time, no one knew what caused it or how to avoid it. Parents were frantic with worry and for good reason in that it mainly affected young children. Some people did survive the disease but most were left with some sort of permanent paralysis in an arm or leg. Many spent the reminder of their life encased in an iron lung. School children from all over the country, as we did at Brandon, raised money one dime at a time through the March of Dimes program to try and find a cure for this disease. I remember on at least two occasions our teacher explaining why one of our classmates would not return because he had died from polio. A few years after leaving Brandon I was one of hundreds who stood in line to receive a lump of sugar saturated with a vaccine which prevented polio. Thank God for Dr. Jonas Salk and the teachers in his life who inspired him.

The most awaited time of the school day for most of us was recess. We had no gym to play indoors but we had a lot of ground outside to rip and run for about thirty minutes in good weather.   The playgrounds at Brandon were segregated based on gender and grade. Girls were restricted to certain areas and boys were restricted to others with no mingling allowed.   A major perk for being a fifth or sixth grader was you were allowed to play on the big field, the one farthest from the school. An area that seemed so immense to young eyes was in reality much smaller when viewed as an adult. But that is true with a lot of things. On the low, far corner of the big field, adjacent to unpaved Aetna Street lived the school custodians, a black man named Payton and his wife. We never knew if Payton was his first or last name, everybody just called him Payton. The old house was still there when I left Brandon and I never knew what became of the people, or the house. Their old house would have been only a few feet from the four-lane Parkway that has split East Florence and caused the area to lose its identity.

One of the great adventures of my young life occurred when I was in the fourth grade. As I said earlier, the older white, wooden frame building was still in place and was fully in use. This building sat directly behind the newer brick building with only a few feet separating the two. It had three levels with the middle floor being level with the ground at the front of the building and that was where the main entrance was located. My fourth grade teacher was Mrs. Floyd and her room was on this level with a row of very large windows running the entire length of the room. Because of the outside slope of the ground, the windows near the front of the room were much closer to the ground than those in the rear of the room. Right outside the door to her room was an anteroom where we were to hang our coats before entering the main room. Most teachers conducted class with their door closed. This made it difficult for gawkers on both sides of the door to practice their craft. On this one particular day, we were sitting in class and smoke began drifting into the room from around the door. Mrs. Floyd opened the door to see what was going on and saw flames engulfing the coats in the anteroom. We had gone through many fire drills that year because the building was so old and made of wood and was a fire hazard. However, all of the drills involved us quickly exiting the building through the front door with no thought of being trapped. She shut the door and ordered all of us to the windows near the front of the room that were closest to the ground, with the girls in front of the line. Proper decorum was to be used at all times, even when the building was burning. We began bailing out those windows like rats from a sinking ship and the entire class escaped unscathed. Nobody ever explained what caused the fire but I had a theory. We had been at recess earlier and some of the boys were prone to take a quick smoke while they could hide outside. When recess ended, maybe a cigarette was hurriedly stuck in a coat pocket without making sure it was properly extinguished and the result was a fire that could have easily ended in tragedy. The ensuing caravan of fire trucks and police cars made the day quite an event in the life of a fourth grader.

Those who study such things tell us that several witnesses to the same event tend to give vastly differing accounts of what happened. No doubt there are many others whose memories of Brandon are far different than mine and so be it. My years at that school were very pleasant and I appreciate the path those teachers made every effort to place within my grasp. After all, that is ultimately what life is about, finding the right path.

Road Trips

During most of my childhood my daddy owned a Packard automobile. It was built sometime around the early 1950's and had a twelve cylinder engine. I suppose the fact that gas was selling for about twenty cents a gallon made it possible to drive such a monstrosity. The Packard Company did not survive the 1950's and, oddly enough, the downfall was not due to fuel inefficiency. Instead, it was severely hurt during the war years because it was not able to obtain enough steel since most of it was going toward the war effort. If a fellow set out to build a Packard, the one thing he would have to have a lot of would be steel. Those old cars had five times the amount of steel as today's cars have plastic and would outweigh them by thousands of pounds.

Today, folks get in their cars and drive to places like Birmingham or Nashville just to eat out or go shopping. We think nothing of driving to Atlanta and back in the same day to watch the Braves play. This was not true when I was a kid. On rare occasions my daddy announced we were going to visit my mother's uncle who lived on Lookout Mountain, near Chattanooga, Tennessee. This was a really big deal for us and a time to celebrate because my family rarely left our home town. The few trips we took were always those that could be made to our destination and back home in a single day. To make the round trip in one day we had to leave home well before dawn and we never arrived back home until very late at night. There was no way my daddy could afford to take his whole family anywhere and spend the night.

Looking back on these trips, there are several things that puzzle me. First, I have always wondered how all of us fit into one car? Despite its size, the capacity of the old Packard was put to a test. My parents, my mother's sister Mary Ellen, my brother Johnny and I and our sister Virginia, who was known all over the community by both relatives and non-relatives as Sis, and almost always one of my sister's

W. E. McDonald proudly sits behind the wheel of his early 1950's Packard.

girlfriends, made the trip. That was seven people in one car. Thank goodness my older brothers were in the military and were not available. Our family was not the kind to spend money along the way so the tourism industry did not benefit from any of our trips. My daddy was a carpenter and loved to build things out of wood. Now, the trunk of his Packard looked like it could almost hold a complete bedroom suite so he had plenty of space to fill. Daddy built a wooden contraption that fit into the trunk and when folded out turned into a table. This was for the purpose of stopping at our convenience and enjoying a sit down meal to eat all the food our mother had prepared. To complement the table he also built several wooden fold-out chairs. The table and food kept us from having to go anywhere near any place that sold food. For some reason, he refused to take advantage of the dozens of roadside pull offs with accompanying picnic tables located only a few miles apart between our house and our destination. In addition to the portable table and some chairs, the trunk always held a huge drink cooler with the words, Dr. Pepper, embossed in large print on each side. It also had a neat little bottle opener built into one end. This thing was made totally of metal. It had double walls for insulation and a metal lid under which rested a metal tray to keep food out of the ice. When fully loaded with drinks, meals and ice it weighed close to a hundred pounds. The only necessity Daddy was not able to cram into the Packard was a toilet and I am certain he gave that idea considerable thought. A lesser automobile would not have been able to make the trip up the steep mountain grades with all the paraphernalia my daddy stuffed into the trunk and with seven people loaded inside. How did it do it? The motto for the Packard Company was, "Ask the Man Who Owns One." Those words said it all for a lot of Packard fans.

The second question inspired by hindsight is how in the world we were able to make the trip safely with the tires Daddy had on the car? Rubber must have still been in short supply for civilian tires because WWII had only recently ended and the Korean War was gaining steam. These factors may have priced new tires out of reach for a lot of people. The tires my daddy ran on his cars were always as slick as the outside of a watermelon. He kept an equally slick spare in the trunk but it was frequently flat when we really needed it, which was often. Flat tires were no big deal. A handy hand pump was also stowed in the trunk and my brother and I were always assigned the chore of inflating tires by pumping furiously on the handle. A blow-out was another problem altogether. This involved actually jacking the car into the air and replacing the bad tire with the semi-bad tire from the trunk. This was not a simple or safe chore on the narrow two lane roads of that time. Daddy always carried a tube patching kit for the times when neither tire would hold air. This arduous task involved breaking the tire down from the wheel, extracting the tube, finding the leak and applying the patch, sometimes with the aid of a flashlight and then reversing the whole process.

One of the best Christmas gifts I remember my daddy ever receiving was a new set of tires for the old car. As a mere youngster, I wasn't privy to the exact details but I believe they were given to him by all my older siblings who had jobs and pooled their money. However, they chose a somewhat unusual and dangerous method to deliver their present and I remember vividly the night the gift arrived unannounced. Our old home place was located in a low area that was once a gulley that drained water from the surrounding hills. Some of my brothers took the tires to the hill above our house and rolled them down the hill onto our front porch. We were sitting in the living room watching the Jack Benny show on a black and white television screen about the size of one of our daddy's empty King Edward cigar boxes when a series of loud crashing sounds came from the front of the house. Daddy always kept a loaded .38 caliber revolver nearby, either in his belt or within arm's reach. As a matter of fact, I always cautioned him on Christmas Eve not to mistake Santa for a prowler and shoot him. So, with gun in hand he opened the front door to discover his Christmas gift lying on the porch. It would have been a shame if he had put a hole in one of the first new tires he had ever owned before he could wear it out on his car.

The roads in use back during my childhood were narrow, full of curves and hills and dangerous to navigate. Our trips to visit our uncle took us through virtually every small hamlet and town in the northern part of the state. I remember with graphic detail the dozens of old barns we passed with the words SEE ROCK CITY painted in white on a black roof. To our dismay, we never saw Rock City, nor did we ever see Ruby Falls which was advertised in much the same manner on a thousand bird houses along the way. Another very impressive Chattanooga attraction we never got to actually experience was the railroad incline,

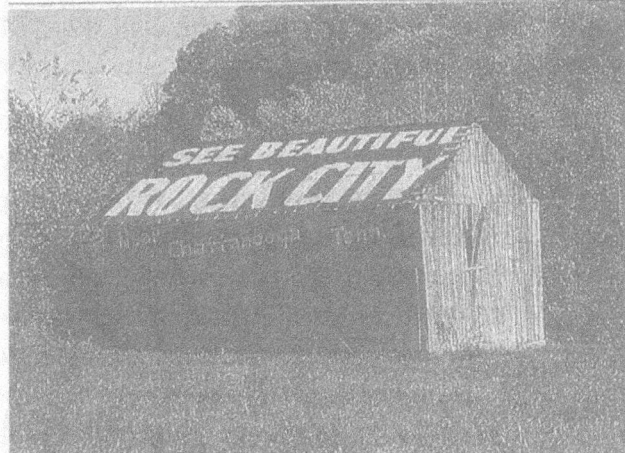

Thousands of these barn signs were scattered across the Southeast luring folks to Lookout Mountain in Chattanooga. Age and highway expansion have done away with most of these relics from the 1940's and 1950's.

which went straight up Lookout Mountain. It was fascinating and scary to watch those railroad cars inch up the mountain but Daddy said it was too expensive for us to ride so we just stood at the top and watched. Another thing I remember about these trips is the number of cars stopped on the way up the mountains with hoods raised and radiators boiling over producing so much steam it looked like they were on fire. Of course, Daddy was prepared for our turn to have to stop because he always kept jugs of water in the trunk. It is strange how those kinds of details remain with me as I grow older but most of the time I can't remember what I had for lunch yesterday.

A more frequent and easier trip we took in the Packard was to visit some of the few remaining relatives of my daddy's mother. They were rather elderly and lived on their farm near Lawrenceburg, Tennessee, which was not all that far from our home. Their old house stood within a few hundred feet of a railroad track which ran from near our home in East Florence to Nashville and beyond.   On many occasions my older brothers had hopped aboard this train and traveled by rail to visit our cousin Nora for several weeks in the summer.   They worked on the farm to earn their keep and were full of tall tales when they returned home. The first television set I ever saw was there in my cousin's house. I remember it had a tiny screen with a very poor picture and was encased in a huge cabinet. I also remember she kept her late husband's Model T Ford on blocks in the barn along with a rifle and a uniform from the Civil War. My brother, Bill, later told me that all these mementoes disappeared gradually over a period of time.

I fast forward the memories of those trips that seemingly took place in slow motion to what my wife and I experience today when we travel. We are blessed to travel in a vehicle accompanied by a pleasant voice determined not to let us get lost and informs us when to turn. Our car has a telephone that allows us to communicate with anyone we wish and never fails to alarm us when it rings unexpectedly.   It even has its own telephone number. We can control the inside temperature at the touch of a button and our radio picks up stations all over the country via satellite. A convenient screen tells us our gas mileage, how much time it will take to reach our destination, how many miles we can expect to travel on the gas remaining in the tank and many other facts which we have no idea how to access.   My daddy would have difficulty believing all of this but would really appreciate the fact that the satellite circling hundreds of miles above the earth will notify us if our tires need air.

This nation is now blessed with literally hundreds of thousands of miles of new and improved roadways. Of course, there are still parts of those old roads left along with a few simple dirt roads meandering through the country side.   Most long distance travelers today use a bustling interstate system crossing mountains, rivers, and prairies with lanes too numerous to count in some large cities. This crown jewel of all our roadways was begun in the 1950's by President Dwight Eisenhower and its ongoing development continues to this very day. In addition to its normal function of moving vehicles rapidly from place to place, the federal roads have been engineered so that designated stretches are flat and straight enough to serve as a runway for airplanes during times of national emergency. So, if you are traveling on an interstate and you witness a fighter jet landing in the next lane, the plane may be experiencing trouble staying aloft or our country is at war and you might need to go home.

One thing I have noticed while traveling these roads is the conflicting nature of some businesses and billboards advertising along the right of way. Some are perfectly logical and the information is useful. For example, it makes good sense to inform travelers about such necessities as food establishments, lodging, churches and gas stations in the miles ahead of you. On the other hand, some of the businesses I have seen make me wonder about the common sense involved in placing something of such questionable nature in a place for the purpose of luring travelers off the roadway. For example, why are so many fireworks stores on these roads? They invariably display names like Crazy Al and Big Daddy on a huge billboard and are spaced every few miles. All claim to have the largest selection of fireworks east of Asia and sell such items as TNT, large rockets the size of a five gallon bucket, and, apparently, actual bombs left over from the last few wars. The puzzling thing about this is why people in so much of a hurry to travel so fast on a super highway actually take the time to stop at these places and shop for explosives which are illegal in many areas? When permits for these businesses are granted, is safety not a consideration? A cigarette in the wrong bin would leave a crater large enough to close down the highway for weeks. The trucks delivering these goods are sort of like torpedoes on wheels. Invariably, right next to the fireworks store is another business which presents a safety issue of its own and, when combined with explosives, quadruples the risk. I am referring to the stores selling fine wines and liquors at discount prices. We know that driving and alcohol don't mix and now we add explosives to the list. What a combination! Load the van up with high explosives, add some cheap Thunderbird and Ripple and try to make up the time lost buying fireworks by doing ninety instead of eighty mph. To add insult to injury, right beside both these businesses is a truck stop where literally hundreds of huge trucks a day stop and the drivers are exposed to the temptation to buy both explosives and liquor. They have in their control a rig that might weigh fifty tons and can be a weapon of mass destruction under the best of conditions. Are terrorists aware that this volatile combination of dangerous products is in such close proximity to major thoroughfares which lead directly to probable targets such as government buildings, hydro-electric dams and major population centers? Why should they bother to smuggle deadly material thousands of miles to get into this country when they can be purchased at a discount alongside our interstates?

As with all good things, as the years passed our family road trips became less and less frequent and were fast becoming nothing but a memory. My sister and her teen-age girlfriends soon found other interests. Eventually, my brother Johnny suffered the same fate. The old Packard gave way to a newer and much smaller Plymouth which didn't have the same appeal as its predecessor. My mother's health began to deteriorate and she did not leave the house much until her death a few years later. That left only Daddy and I at home and road trips with just the two of us didn't seem like a whole lot of fun.

Children and Church

Our church recently hosted a district wide meeting of Methodist laity. After a wonderful meal and good fellowship, we retired to the church sanctuary for the business meeting to be followed by a short message from one of the pastors present. Since we were the host church I stayed and helped clean up the dining area so this made me a little late going upstairs. When I arrived in the sanctuary, it was close to being full, so I took a seat on a back pew. Of course, this was not a regular church service, so the routine was different. However, there was another difference so stark it was immediately noticeable. The make-up of this congregation was unlike any I had ever seen in our church, outside of a funeral. I was looking across a solid sea of gray and white heads. I include myself when I say this was a church full of older people. One reason may have been that younger members are not able to make meetings like this during the work week. Older members are generally more faithful in attending these meetings, maybe because many of us are retired, and we have little else to do. The average age must have been close to seventy, give or take a few years. However, age was not the most noticeable difference. It immediately struck me that there was no noise as we waited for the meeting to begin. There was almost total silence, the sanctuary was eerily silent. It had the atmosphere of a funeral rather than a church service. There was no talking, no laughter, no children moving around making a racket and no babies crying. They say you don't miss your water until the well runs dry and this was a case of not missing noise until there is no noise. Before our regular church services begin the building is full of life with a buzzing beehive of noise. An undertone of talking and laughing and a lot of noise from the children seems to be a regular part of the service. Observing children at church reminds me a lot of when I was raising goats. Now, in no way am I comparing children to goats, even though a baby goat is also called a kid. A kid goat will get so full of itself, it cannot stand still. Suddenly, it will just jump straight up in the air, twisting and turning all the way. It will run around leaping onto anything it can find. It exudes a joy just to be alive that is refreshing to watch. Sometimes, a child at church acts much the same way after sitting still as long as it can.

Certainly, it was not the fault of those of us attending the event that age was creeping up on us. In fact, most of us would have really preferred that not to be the case. On my way home, I thought about how blessed we are to have a wide range of ages in our church. Hopefully, the young can benefit from us older folks and I know having the children around can gladden our hearts with their innocence and exuberance. However, any parents who have taken their children to church on a regular basis know they have had to suffer through painfully embarrassing moments on more than one occasion. Books have been written on some of the things children repeat at church. I know many parents tend to have a panicky feeling when they see their child talking to the pastor and have nightmares about what is being said. In addition to this, the task of just getting them there can be monumental and can't be overlooked. The hurried meals, squabbling, bathing and arranging hair, not to mention clothes, would be enough to stop many of us in our tracks. While most children are a joy most of the time, that joy is not necessarily evident for all those involved in the process of getting them ready for church. These folks certainly deserve a special reward for their perseverance and thick skin. It would behoove us older folks to remember what it was like.

After my experience that night, I am more grateful than ever for the infants, children, teenagers and young adults who are a part of our congregation. The religion we now know as Shakers had a completely different view of a church filled with children and it is quite puzzling to me since it led to their demise as a religion. A basic tenet of their faith demands celibacy, even among married couples. Members could marry but had to live separately. I suppose it was rather easy to detect couples who were not living out their faith. Since there were no little Shakers coming along to add to the church rolls they depended solely on adult converts to perpetuate their beliefs. This policy did not work out well for them. Thankfully, our church is a growing one and not in decline. Jesus recognized the importance of having children as part of worship and scolded the disciples when they tried to prevent the children from coming to Him. When a church is faced with the option, it is far better to have growing pains than to have dying pains. A church with no children is on its deathbed. If you can find a Shaker, just ask him.

My Favorite Aunt

It is a mystery to me how we can live alongside one of God's richest blessings and not even be aware of it at the time. To make it worse, it is generally too late to make amends by the time we come to our senses. This has happened to me more than once in my life and I have prayed many times for God to grant me the wisdom to recognize these situations. My aunt, Mary Ellen Lindsey, was one of the great blessings of my life and I didn't know it. My maternal grandparents, Leonard and Lucy Lindsey, raised nine children and lived just a short distance from our house. Mary Ellen, my mother's sister, was the youngest member of this large family. She was about seventeen years my senior. We were all raised in the little community on the east side of Florence known appropriately as East Florence. Her father, Leonard, owned and operated a small grocery store in the middle of the community and was a staunch Methodist in the local church.

There was no place for Mary Ellen in the public schools of the 1940's and 1950's. She only attended school for a few days and her parents were told to take her home. Today, she would be labeled as challenged, back then she was called retarded and unable to learn. We were told in my family that Mary Ellen was just "slow." My mother felt a special obligation to care for her after our grandparents passed away and she lived with us until my mother died in 1964. For a short period of time she was bounced from one older sister to the next but the love she felt in our home was replaced by resentment and embarrassment and these arrangements failed miserably. After that experiment, the remainder of her life was spent living with paid caretakers and, finally, in a nursing home the last few years of her life.

Even though Mary Ellen was forced to live outside the community she loved and grew up in, East Florence remained her spiritual home. In her mind she could still tromp across the hills and hollows of East Florence and describe every house and the people who lived there. She was a fixture in the community in which she lived and loved to stop and visit with her neighbors. Time did not seem to mean anything to her and, because of this, she was never in a hurry. There were three great loves in her life: her family, her rocking chair and a porch swing. In spite of her raising, she developed a special fondness for Coca-Cola and unfiltered Camels later in life. Since most everyone she knew smoked she was able to bum a smoke without a lot of trouble. However, the cokes were dependent on her being able to cajole one of her nephews or nieces out of some money.

Despite some mental challenges, Mary Ellen was able to remember the birthday of every single member of her family. She never failed to remind us of the upcoming birthday of a brother, sister, spouse, nephew, niece, in-law, or anyone remotely related to her. Mary Ellen did this entirely from memory since she could neither read nor write and did not have the benefit of marking a calendar. One of her favorite stories was how she rocked me when I was a baby and I have vivid memories of us spending countless hours swinging on our front porch while singing and laughing. Being childlike herself, she loved to play with children and we were great friends. But, like many boys, I was prone to pester people and Mary Ellen was a favorite target because she was always around. No matter how mad she got, she would chase after me but we would wind up laughing. In spite of my pranks she was always quick to forgive me and we shared many good times later in life at some of the tricks I pulled on her.

While she was living in the nursing home, Mary Ellen would bubble over with excitement when her family visited. She introduced each of us to the staff on every visit, no matter that we had been there dozens of times before. She would boast to all her friends that she was my favorite aunt and she was right.   It was always a great event for her when her family gathered at the nursing home and celebrated her birthday and other special holidays. Before anyone could leave my sister always had to play the piano while everyone had a sing-a-long.   While the singing might have left a lot to be desired we were

at least making what the Bible refers to as a "joyful noise." When asked what she wanted as a gift for our next visit, she would always reply, "step-ins," which is what women call underwear today.   This made it very easy for her female relatives to shop for her but the same cannot be said for the rest of us. Some of my brothers and I would just pitch in and buy her a carton of Camels and a case of cokes and hope our mother would forgive us.

Tom McDonald with his favorite aunt, Mary Ellen Lindsey.

Aunt Mary Ellen was a very special person in the lives of the McDonald family. Some of her other nieces and nephews seemed to be embarrassed that she was their aunt, but they didn't know what they were missing. Her love for us was far beyond what could be measured and was as

65

close to unconditional love as could be found in this cruel world. This kind of love had to be close to what Jesus meant when he told us to love our neighbor. We should have carved the thirteenth chapter of First Corinthians on her tombstone. In many ways Mary Ellen was able to go through her life and never abandon the joy of childhood. The challenges she faced were lost in the delight she found in her family and friends. As is the case many times, I was in too big of a hurry and considered many other things to be too important to appreciate the extent of that love and did not take the time to return nearly enough of it. Only later in my life did I finally realize how wrong I had been and what a gift from God she was, and I feel blessed she was such a big part of my life.

Like Father, Like Son

One thing we learn, hopefully, as we grow older, is that some things have to be done whether we want to do them or not. There is no doubt one of the many joys of Heaven will be the absence of boring, sweaty, arduous tasks. In the meantime, life goes on down here on earth. Many young folks consider it "unfair" to be burdened with chores that interfere with the more pleasant activities of their lives. That was the same reaction for my generation as well as for those stretching back as far as we can remember. I have always found it amusing that many of these young folks expect to be paid to do chores around the house and even to make good grades in school. What is even more amazing is that many parents actually fall for this con game and pay their children to do what is expected of them.   My father would find this practice astonishing, to say the least. He firmly believed, and practiced, the theory that work is good for the soul and, it seemed, there was always a revival in progress at our house. Out of necessity, he learned to do virtually everything for himself. During the Great Depression, with a young family, he lost his job and his house and lived in a tent for two years.   Because of this and other difficult experiences, he believed hiring others to do tasks he could do on his own was something he could ill afford and never got into that habit.   A carpenter by trade, he was above average at plumbing, electrical work, painting, sheet metal work, roofing and masonry work.   Any unskilled labor, such as digging was left to his brood of six sons.   As my brothers left home, all the digging was soon delegated to me. Even today it seems every chore on my list involves digging. It was also my responsibility to be his helper, to hold things, to go get a tool for him, to go with him on jobs in our neighborhood and do whatever was needed. Although he was small in stature, I believed there was nothing my father could not do. He did his best to pass along these skills to his six sons because he always thought bad times were around the corner and being as independent as possible was a necessity for survival.   He found plenty for us to do and expected it to be done without him having to follow along behind. If we did something that did not meet his expectations, we had to do it over and get it right.

Our daddy was a strict disciplinarian but he loved us deeply and we knew it. I was a teenager during the 1960's, or as some called these years, the Age of Aquarius. This was the time of free love when thousands of young men and women left their roots to go out into the world and "find themselves." They traveled to far off places to sit at the feet of some mystic in the mountains of Nepal to learn the real truth about life. If they didn't go that far, they probably wound up in San Francisco smoking dope on the streets. As far as I know, none of my siblings, and certainly not me, ever knew we should be out looking because we already knew who we were. If we had any questions about the situation, I have no doubt that our daddy would tell us the answer.

This philosophy of life worked so well for my father I decided to keep the tradition going. My wife and I were blessed with two children and they grew up knowing how to do physical labor. This is not an inherited trait, it has to be learned. They didn't necessarily enjoy the work they just did it without excessive complaining. One day we were in the garden picking up the potatoes I had plowed up with my tractor.   This is always tedious, backbreaking work and the rows must have looked to be a mile long to our son, Will.   He had a long, unpleasant day but the experience of that day, and others like it, paid off for him. The value of self -discipline helped to make him the fine man he turned out to be. On many occasions when Will was young, I tried to pass along some particular bit of information that would be useful later in his life. I would say things in a certain way and it was easy to tell he was determined not to listen. Much to my surprise, he was paying attention but didn't want me to know. I know that to be true because he told me so years later, after he married and had a family of his own. There are times today, listening to him talk to his sons that I can hear myself talking to him. Even more astonishing, I can hear my father talking to me. Is this where the phrase, "Like father, like son," comes from?

As I get older I worry that I was unreasonable with my children. There is no doubt I made many, many mistakes and they come back to haunt me like snapshots in my mind. When I wonder what I would do differently if I had my life to live over, the answer is simple. I would not spend my time looking for a better job that paid more money with which to buy a lot of stuff, or more prestige or a larger house. Time spent seeking the temporary things of this world to the detriment of what is truly important is wasted and accomplishes nothing but to cause us more stress. It is a shame it usually takes us so long to come to that conclusion. I would ask God for less pride and more patience, understanding, tolerance and a lot more time spent with my children. And, most importantly of all, I would spend a lot of time kneeling at the bedside of my children praying with them over matters they were dealing with in their lives and worry less about what I thought was important in my life. This is the only way to create true wealth.

Whistlers

My wife and I were visiting our son and his family a while back and it was fast approaching time for our two grandsons to come home for supper. Now, these are pretty big boys and they are prone to wander far and wide in the neighborhood. I was curious as to just how their mother was going to get them to come home because she didn't know where they were.   The neighborhood was far too genteel and sophisticated for her to go out in the yard and start yelling at the top of her lungs. I am sure that would violate some provision of the local homeowners' association code of conduct. These dictator inspired committees are common in up-scale neighborhoods and can actually tell homeowners what they can and can't do on their own property. Besides, her two sons would consider her behavior to be uncouth as they have reached the age where being suave is very important.   Shame is rained on their head when a parent does something to attract unwanted attention and their lives are forever ruined. Some older farmhouses in our neighborhood had a bell on a pole outside the house that was used to call workers in from the fields or even to signal an emergency in the community.   My wife and I used this method at times to summon our own children and it worked quite well as long as you have a bell.   However I am sure the same bunch of homeowners would have some sort of prohibition against bells ringing as well.   Instead of doing any of these things she simply picked up her cell phone, dialed a number and said to whoever answered, "Come home, it's time to eat." This is more evidence that I have no place in today's technology based society. Within a few minutes they thundered through the door, ready to eat. Pavlov would have been proud.

This got me to thinking about how it was when I was growing up and our daddy needed any of us to come home. He had a way of calling his seven children that was unique and didn't involve a cell phone or a bell.   Instead, he put two fingers in his mouth and whistled in a very loud, shrill tone that could be heard from far away. What made it unique was that he had a different whistle for each of his seven children.   Those hearing the sound for the first time would only hear a shrill whistle and it would make no sense. However, not only could his kids identify their whistle but our neighbors soon learned who was being called and would tell us our daddy was calling for us to come home.   This was very helpful on their part because Daddy had what would be called today, a zero tolerance policy. If we failed to appear within a time he considered to be reasonable, he jumped to one of two possible conclusions, neither of them good. We had either ignored his whistle or we were too far from home to hear it and we were guilty until proven innocent.

In addition to calling his children with his whistle, my daddy was just what some would call, "a whistling man." He whistled when he worked and at other times just for the sheer joy of it. Whistling is cheap, clean and requires no instrument or knowledge of music. People whistle for a variety of reasons. Like my daddy, they whistle to get someone's attention or to express their emotions. I am proud to say that I am a whistler like my father and my son also whistles a lot. Recently, I was very pleased to learn that our oldest grandson is carrying on the family tradition and has taken up the art of whistling. It seems to be sort of a man thing because I can't ever remember hearing a woman whistle, although our daughter can whistle when pressured. I suppose if you grow up around a whistler you are more prone to pick up the habit. The art of whistling goes way back and I have read it was mentioned in some writings as early as the fourteenth century. Whistling has even become a part of our vocabulary with expressions such as, "wolf whistle," or "clean as a whistle," or "whistling Dixie," and "whistling past a graveyard."

A fellow that my daddy did some work for one time was not able to pay him with money, so he gave him a big parrot that could wolf whistle better than any man I ever heard. Unfortunately, many of the women who walked past our house thought one of us was whistling at them. It took a good while to straighten out the situation.

Overall, I think people like whistlers as a rule. Whether it's true or not, people who whistle have the reputation of being happy, unless they are constantly whistling funeral dirges. Most people, I believe, enjoy listening to other people whistle even if they don't whistle themselves. I often whistle while walking and many times total strangers will take the time to compliment me. My favorite whistling tunes are old church hymns and folk songs but virtually any song will do as long as you know the melody. Word memorization is not necessary to be a competent whistler.

It seems to me that the world would be a better place if more people took up whistling. It won't solve any problems but it seems to put them out of mind for a while. I have heard it said about some people that they can't walk and chew gum at the same time. Whether that is true or not, I don't claim to know, but it would be a predicament. However, I do know that you can't whistle and worry about your problems at the same time. So, if we have to choose between whistling and worrying, why not choose whistling? If people think you are happy then maybe that will help them feel a little better about their problems. With the advent of the twenty-four hour news cycle that never ends and cell phones that won't allow us to escape, bad news is always just a click away. If whistling can carry us safely past a graveyard at night, maybe it can bring us just a few minutes reprieve from our worries.

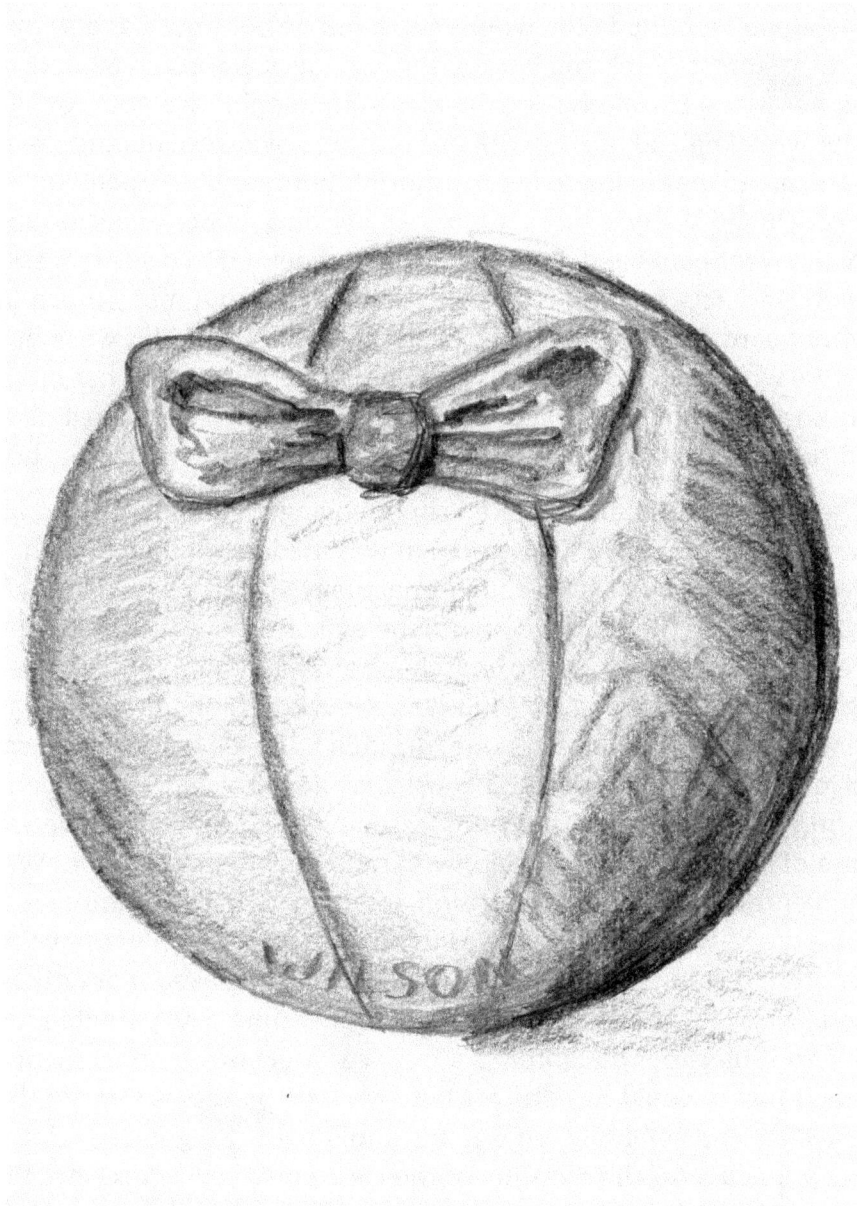

Charm School

    Our daughter was born a tomboy. It was evident from her behavior when she was only a toddler. She loved horses, dogs and cats and was a magnet for lost and abandoned

animals. She whopped around in the woods surrounding our house and swung on vines.
She waded across Cypress Creek and walked through thick woods and a dark, snaky creek
bottom to visit her friend Elizabeth. She did play with her girl toys occasionally but
seemed happier wrestling and boxing with her brother. We were hoping she would take
an interest in the piano that belonged to my mother but that didn't pan out. After months
of lessons we concluded she was more interested in riding horses and shooting skeet. Her
attire was mostly sweat pants and a tee shirt and she seemed to disdain dresses. As I
recall, there were very few pretend tea parties at our house but many touch football
games in the front yard and basketball games in the back yard.   This was not a problem
for us because we were certain she would grow out of it. We signed her up to play
softball when she was seven. She loved the position of catcher because it allowed her to
grovel in the dirt and hopefully knock down any runner attempting to steal home.

       In the seventh grade she considered cheerleading for a nano-second before
deciding basketball was her game. This decision was made after watching the women play
basketball during the Olympics.   Our daughter actually played in the first real basketball
game she had ever seen.   The first two points she ever scored was a lay-up resulting from
an incredibly exciting fast break. Unfortunately, she scored them for the other team and
her coach began calling her 'wrong way.'   It was about this time her mother and I, looking
for a problem where there really wasn't one, decided to enroll her in charm school. An ad
had appeared in the local paper advertising just such a school and we decided it couldn't
do her any harm.   Actually, she already possessed plenty of charm but we were hoping
to temper some of her tomboyish behavior with more ladylike demeanor. We felt it best
to go ahead and enroll her for the next session and pay the tuition before we revealed our
plan to her. To say she was not pleased was to put it mildly. Our persuasive powers were
put to a rather stern test but, we insisted she go whether she liked it or not. For a while
her mother and I were afraid she might run away from home. As parents are prone to do
we were willing to subject our daughter to a fate we would never inflict on ourselves
under the pretext that it would be good for her. My wife picked her up at school on the
day she had the class and generally ran errands until time to go get her. Her mood could
be described as very dark for the duration of the class and a few weeks into the term we
began to fear we had made a big mistake. A phone call from the instructor informing us
our daughter had been expelled from charm school would not have been a surprise.
Thankfully, the call never came.   We concluded our money had been wasted on the day
my wife was waiting outside to pick her up and our daughter came walking from the
opposite direction eating ice cream. Surely she wasn't cutting class at charm school.   She
stuck to the story that class ended early that day. Her final grade was a 'c' which we think
was the only such grade she made her entire life.   Apparently, the instructor graded on

the curve and had different expectations from certain students. Afterwards, we couldn't see any discernible difference so we never mentioned it again.

She stuck with basketball and her skill as a player improved to the point she was able to attend college on an athletic scholarship, which greatly pleased us. The money we saved by not having to pay college tuition more than made up for her charm school expenses. College exposed her to sorority girls which she and her teammates referred to as 'bowheads', apparently from the colorful bows they wore in their hair. The social activities associated with sorority and fraternity life in college were totally contradictory to her mode of operation. This went on for a couple of years until one day we were caught completely off guard. It is said that the college experience changes people in strange ways and we found it to be very true. She informed us that she had been invited to join a sorority and was going to accept the invitation. Finally, her stint at charm school was showing results, although greatly delayed.

George, the Donkey

Over the years, we have provided a home for a variety of goats, from purebred Nubians, to fainting goats, to scrubby bush goats. For those who are not familiar with goats, a fainting or nervous goat has a genetic defect in the central nervous system which causes it to literally faint, or pass out, when frightened. This makes them extremely vulnerable to predators and young children who have a devious and disturbed sense of humor. Goats can provide a lot of entertainment, especially young ones, but there is also a downside. They easily succumb to parasites and are prone to have crippling foot problems. Also, the bane of every person with goats is the predators they seem to attract, namely dogs and coyotes. A coyote will snatch a young goat for a meal and his only concern is to escape and enjoy the feast. On the other hand, a pack of domesticated dogs will destroy an entire herd if not stopped. Most people refuse to believe their family pet, Fido, would have any part in killing anything, much less a goat. By himself, he probably wouldn't, but with a pack of other dogs a family pet can display unbelievable savagery. So, having lost dozens of goats to dogs over the years, I decided to buy a male donkey, or jack, to run with them. A jack will attempt to kill any animal it considers a predator. It is extremely territorial and a deadly border enforcer. He will use his teeth and hooves very effectively as deadly weapons. This probably dates back to times past when they were forced to defend themselves against all kinds of wild critters. The jack has no particular fondness for goats, or cattle, or horses, it is just reacting to some inherited instinct for survival. Consequently, many people pasture a jack with their herd animals.

A fellow not far from us had a sign in his yard advertising donkeys for sale. He did have one jack in his barn that was normal in size. All the others were large and called mammoth jacks. The smaller jack was about the size of a burro you see in the movies. The old fellow called him George and this seemed to be an appropriate name. He assured me that George had run with goats in the past, which was very important. A jack unaccustomed to goats might consider them to be a predator and the results would be catastrophic to the goats. So, when George placed his head against my chest and sort of nuzzled me, the deal was sealed.

George and I became fast friends from the very outset. He was soon following me around with his head almost touching my back and was very gentle and affectionate. At times, George would stand on the hill with an excellent view of our house. He would stare at the house for hours and bray until I came out. It was kind of like a kid standing in my yard waiting for me to come out and play. My wife found this practice to be very annoying. George was actually valuable to me in another way. Anytime my wife used the word 'jackass', there was always the possibility she was referring to him and not me. This was not the case before George took up residence. Our friendship reached such a high level that I sold all my goats to concentrate on donkeys. Donkeys were much friendlier and took care of themselves, not like goats. Another thing about donkeys is that they will treat you as an equal. Dogs are always acting subservient and cats act superior as if it is painful for them to have to be in your presence for any reason other than to be fed.

Since donkeys are a herd animal, it seemed to be a good idea for George to have some company. Soon, two jennets, or female donkeys, joined our small herd. This seemed to make George very happy. His previous owner had used him as a 'teaser'. A teaser is a small stud, like a donkey or a pony, too short to actually breed a normal size mare. His purpose was to 'tease' the female until she was ready to breed. Further details are probably not necessary to fully explain how this works. His previous employment made it quite understandable why George acted in such an aggressive manner around the jennets. A period of adjustment was going to be necessary in order to get his mind out of the gutter. Therefore, George was put in his stall when the jennets arrived and he had only visual contact with his new friends. He did look askance at me once or twice as if to ask, "why?" The females were allowed to roam freely while George looked on in frustration.

The jennets had been on the scene for several days when our daughter arrived to visit for the weekend. She teaches school in another part of the state and had invited a colleague and her twelve year old daughter to come along with her to our house in the country. Our daughter was raised around farm animals and had a good grasp of what some call, strangely enough, the birds and the bees. However, her friends were dyed in the wool city folks. Any knowledge they might have had regarding this topic was not made known to me as it was actually none of my business. They came to enjoy a few days in the country and, especially, to see the donkeys.

Their presence sort of forced my hand on the decision as to when to release George. Timing is a big part of life. The Bible speaks of a time to live and a time to die, a time to eat and a time to fast and a time to celebrate and a time to be sorrowful. It soon became apparent this was not the time to turn George out with the jennets. He came out of his stall like a thoroughbred comes out of the starting gate at the Kentucky Derby. A subtle approach was not one of his strong points. The first jennet he laid eyes on received more attention than she wanted. He immediately mounted her with romance on his mind. She responded with a few swift kicks but George was not discouraged by this not so subtle rebuff. At this time, I was a witness to one of the most incredible displays of balance and determination I had seen in my whole life. Our barn is located on a shelf cut into the side of a rather steep hill overlooking a small creek bottom. The hill is by no means a gentle slope to the creek, it drops off rather abruptly. The jennet, with George still aboard, bolted down the hill at a dead gallop. Facing such a challenge, one would expect the normal reaction would be to dismount and hope for a better day. Apparently, George had been frustrated far too long and was expecting some immediate action. As the pair thundered down the hill, the jennet squealing and George braying, they sort of looked like a six legged donkey with two heads. The jennet leveled out at the bottom of the hill, made a quick circuit round the creek bottom, and headed back up the hill toward the barn. George had no input in the route she chose to take since he was in the role of a passenger. With only two feet actually touching the ground he was forced to follow her lead. Apparently, she thought she could scrape him off by going through the barn door, but she was wrong. The pair hit a narrow barn door at full speed with George still attached like a cocklebur. Loud, banging noises ensued from inside the barn and I knew it was not safe to enter. The jennet emerged after a few minutes and, in my book, was clearly the victor. George stayed inside, apparently mending his wounded pride and any other bruises he might have picked up on his wild ride.

It was difficult for me to decide what to say since this entire sorry spectacle took place with George's manhood fully exposed to all the spectators. My wife and daughter were aghast at the events that had unfolded before their very eyes. The twelve year old was staring with open mouth and eyes popping out. This would have been a good opportunity for her mother to at least begin to explain what all parents dread, the birds and bees. The actual scene was less problematic to me than the question and answer session that was bound to follow if I stayed around. I was not prepared to field any inquiries from anyone present and, luckily, there were other chores needing my immediate attention for the remainder of the day and far into the night. As for George, he got along nicely with his new friends after that one episode.

Teachers

I remember vividly my very first encounter with a school teacher. The only thing I had known about teachers and schools came from the mouths of my five older brothers and sister. In their infinite wisdom, they assured me that all teachers had fangs and devoured little children. On my very first day of school, my mother, perhaps giddy from the knowledge the last of her seven children had finally reached school age, sent me under the capable guidance of my next oldest brother, Johnny, who was in the fourth grade. As did all of our siblings, parents, and grandparents before us, we walked from our house to the front door of Brandon School in East Florence. The enormity of what was happening to me had finally kicked in and I refused to go any further. Suddenly, school had no place in my future and I was ready to go back home to the good life. My brother, who had already fulfilled his responsibility to take me to school, realized the embarrassment involved in dragging a screaming younger brother into the building, quickly fled the scene and went for help. Very soon, a lady appeared and introduced herself as my teacher. Her name was Mrs. Nadine Sullivan and I will never forget her. She sat beside me on the front step of the school and began to talk about how much fun we would have learning new things in her class. Most of all, she convinced me she was glad I was to be in her room. She soon had me downstairs helping her with chairs, tables and bulletin boards. I remember that teacher, and others who came along later, because they cared about me. Students can quickly determine which teachers really care and that makes all the difference in the world. I remember my own children and the way they mentioned certain teachers. They didn't spend any time talking with their friends about new technology or new teaching methods or new textbooks. They talked about which teacher they wanted to have next year.

My career in education began in 1968 and ended with my retirement in November, 1999, just a few weeks shy of bridging portions of five decades. Early in my teaching career, I spent one miserable year as an assistant principal in a junior high school. It was true then and it is true today, assistant principals are assigned those duties, which in the military might be referred to as "latrine duty." Any duty which involved leaving the school for a downtown luncheon with a civic club or, especially, traveling out of town to frequent workshops was quickly gobbled up by the principal. Assistants are always given odious duties such as discipline and attendance but even these duties often provide humorous moments. It wasn't all bad. While monitoring attendance, I also had to keep track of those late for school or for a particular class. Our school was located downtown and many of our students had to walk or ride with parents if they were not eligible to ride the bus.

Each morning, to keep the office from being clogged with late students, I set up a table in the hall just inside the main entrance. All students arriving late had to report to me in order to receive a pass to enter class. I honestly tried to be objective as each student explained why they were late getting to school. Realistically, some students were late because of their parents and I tried to take that into consideration in my role as judge, jury and executioner. One eighth grade girl, we'll call her Wanda, was late constantly. We had basically the same conversation almost every morning. It went something like this, "O, K. Wanda, why are you late today?" She was very creative in conjuring up new excuses and would have made a good living spinning the truth for a politician. She either overslept or had to spend the night with her grandmother or it was raining or the alarm clock was broken or her little brother was sick or they couldn't get the car started or the car had a flat tire, etc., etc., etc. Soon, I began to use the word, "negligent" when I responded to her excuse for the day. My sermon was pretty much a canned speech and Wanda knew it by heart. It went something like, "Wanda, the bottom line is that you are simply negligent. You should go to bed earlier, get a new clock, wake up earlier," and on and on. In spite of my best lectures, she continued to be late. On one particular day, Wanda came strolling in the door, late as usual. As she drew nearer to my table, I could see she was desperately trying to come up with a new excuse. Her brain was thumbing through her mental Rolodex, to no avail. After giving me time to make my opening remarks, she finally got going. "Mr. Mac, I, uh, uh, I was just uh, uh, uh, Mr. Mac my uh, uh," and then the truth finally came forth, "Mr. Mac, I was just plain negligent today." I never did get her to come to school on time but I was successful in helping her add a new word for her vocabulary.

One of my most unpleasant responsibilities as an assistant principal was to be in charge of all discipline in the school. It didn't take long for me to decide which teachers were able to control their students and which could not. The teachers who had the respect of their students rarely had a problem serious enough to warrant my attention. Much of my time was spent dealing with problems that should never have occurred or should have been dealt with in the classroom by the teacher. While dealing with these problems, I often thought back to my elementary teachers and remembered how they handled unruly students in their class. First off, elementary teachers in the 1950's could be likened to feudal barons of the Middle Ages. Their word was law and was not to be disputed. Pity the poor ACLU attorney who attempted to convince these ladies that reading the Bible to students was a violation of the Constitution of the United States of America. Since I did not attend church, my first and only information about Biblical characters came from these teachers who insisted we learn about them. They read to us about the faith of Daniel as he faced the lions, about Moses who defied the mighty Pharaoh and about Joseph who forgave his brothers even though they sold him into slavery. They did it in such a manner that a bunch of hard headed boys hung onto every word.

Old school buildings of that time had a small, narrow room which ran clear across the back of the room called the cloak room. Since most of us walked to school, this room was a repository for coats, rubber boots, rain coats, gloves and other types of outer wear we had to wear in inclement weather but did not need around us in class. It served a dual purpose in that it was often used as an interrogation room for those suspected of violating any rule of civilized society the teacher felt should not be violated. Wide latitude was always given in such matters and it was often left solely to the interpretation of the teacher to gauge the severity of the offense. Teachers in that day had no concept of the due process rights of students and some of their techniques would have made water boarding seem about as harmful as bobbing for apples. When the questioning ended, the privacy of the cloak room allowed the perpetrator to be punished beyond the prying eyes of classmates eager to see a hanging. Even with absolutely no legal training, the conviction rate was pretty high. Those leaving the dreaded cloak room with a rare reprieve knew to tread lightly because there was no such thing as double jeopardy. However, those days are long gone.

During the period of time I spend in education, monumental changes occurred in our schools. Some were good and some not so good with the majority of the negative ones being brought about by changes in society, specifically the family. More than any other institution in our society, our schools have had to shoulder the burden of filling in the gaps in the lives of children that the family normally provided in the past. This tremendous responsibility has resulted in many of our public schools teetering on the edge of collapse. This shift has been well documented by scholars, media news outlets and has been the subject of scores of books. Teacher training institutions have revamped curricula and teaching methods many times and the technology involved has evolved from chalkboards to classroom computers hooked up worldwide and laptops replacing traditional textbooks. Technology has allowed students from small rural schools with limited course offerings to have university lectures brought live to their class. When I began my teaching career, we were proud to have an overhead projector that worked and someone to clean our chalkboard erasers. Any machine we borrowed from the library to show our class the latest sixteen millimeter film invariably had a burned out bulb.

In spite of all these changes, the human element, not technology, is the most important factor in teaching. A teacher who teaches students instead of a subject out of a book will always be successful. Teachers are no different from other folks, some are bright, others not so bright. Over the years, I have worked with hundreds of teachers, from kindergarten to high school. Some have been world class teachers and others have been mediocre at best with many leaving the classroom for a wide variety of reasons. The art of evaluating teachers has gone through more than its share of changes, from simple observation by an administrator to paperwork that stifles the whole process. Some have asked me what qualities, in my opinion, make some educators successful and others not able to cope. One has to begin with the fact education has been a political football in this state, and many other states, for as long as I can remember. Our schools are faced with a constant barrage of criticism from the media, apathy from many in the general public and incredible lack of appreciation from many elected leaders. The number of politicians who have waged a campaign for a public office solely on the promise to improve our schools increases with the political seasons. Every new governor and legislature that comes along introduces a new opinion about how to evaluate schools and teachers and the entire process starts over from scratch. Because of this, teachers have a tendency to circle the wagons and view the world through cynical eyes. The truth is teachers in our public schools have absolutely no control over their situation. They have to take the students as they are sent to them and do the best they can. This is not necessarily the case in most private schools where students who persist in bad behavior can be sent packing at the drop of a hat. Teachers have never had any control over the policy decisions that have such a major impact over how they are able to do their jobs. The actual policy makers never come near a student or a classroom. All these factors tend to build up and cause even very good teachers to become cynical and suffer what is called teacher burn out. One of the oddities of the field of education is that the farther the employee is removed from the kids, the higher their salary. This frequently takes the best teachers out of the classroom and promotes them to non-teaching positions where they can make more money but students are deprived of their outstanding teaching ability. Furthermore, success in the classroom does not always translate to success in a supervisory role.

Be that as it may, I believe there are some common factors that separate successful teachers from the rest of their colleagues. The problem is the things I feel are most important cannot be measured like politicians want to do. Certainly, knowledge of subject matter is important and can be measured. But, it is impossible to measure an individual's ability to convey that knowledge to others. However, in my opinion, this is not the most important factor. Instead, I believe successful teachers have an 'aura' about them that cannot be measured. Aura is defined as a "distinctive air or atmosphere." This aura causes students to listen, to behave and to respect the teacher. Without this atmosphere a teacher spends more time trying to keep control of a class than actually teaching the students in that class. When this occurs, knowledge of subject matter is out the window and becomes almost a non-factor.

Equally important, I believe, is a sense of humor. This does not mean the teacher should be the classroom jester because there are enough students to fill that role. The fact is that many high school students can be very funny and their sense of humor can frequently add a lot to a class if not allowed to get out of control. The ability to laugh at oneself and laugh with, not at, students is necessary for survival. A lot of funny things happen in the classroom and a teacher who is too stiff and unbending to laugh at something obviously funny has little or no credibility with the students. To put it bluntly, some teachers take themselves far too seriously. When our daughter began her student teaching several years ago, I told her two things were absolutely essential to be successful. One, never park in another teacher's parking place. I have seen eager young teachers summoned to the office over the public address system and told to move their vehicle. Two, never sit in another teacher's seat in the cafeteria. These seats are as closely guarded as church pews. Avoid these two things and the rest is a piece of cake. Flexibility, not rigidity, is the key. Schools corral hundreds of young people together in one place and this is a recipe for drama. Successful teachers work around the daily disruptions and are not stymied by them. Believe me, if the funny stories passed around in the teacher's lounge were ever collected and put into print, a best seller would be inevitable.

Much of the humor comes from technology gone awry or from technology used without thinking. An exciting advancement from just a few years back is the source of a lot of funny stories among teachers. The public address system replaced the archaic system of having to send notes from the office when administrators needed to communicate with teachers or students. However, it is almost as annoying as the knock on the door to fetch someone to the office. The most carefully crafted lesson plan is probably interrupted more than once each hour during most days. Invariable, right in the middle of something very important in the classroom, the speaker blares forth with a trivial announcement that means very little to most folks. The speaker can also provide a great deal of entertainment when the person using the device doesn't realize how they come across in the ears of those listening.

My wife worked as a library aide at a very small school in a rural area of the county. The principal was quick on the trigger to just pick up the mike and say whatever crossed his mind that he thought everybody needed to hear. One day he embarrassed himself and the physical education teacher with just such an announcement. It seems some of the junior high boys were bringing footballs and softballs to play with during recess. As usually happens, it didn't take long for the halls to be filled with boys throwing balls back and forth to each other. To rectify this, the principal announced to the whole school, "You boys need to stop bringing those balls to school. Go down to the gym and see Coach, he's got enough balls for all of you to play with." Needless to say, the coach had to have a thick skin for a good while to put up with all the jokes he had to endure.

Believe it or not, a speaker that is not working is also able to cause quite an uproar in a crowd of students. An accepted fact of life in most schools is that the heat will not work in cold weather and the air conditioning will not work in hot weather. It cannot be explained but that is just the way it works. When the school public address system goes on the blink at the same time bad things tend to occur. One day at our school, the heat was not working, it was very cold outside and the speaker was malfunctioning. Workers were frantically trying to get heat to the various wings of the school. The main office, unable to communicate with any of the rooms to determine which areas were still without heat, was trying to keep abreast of the situation as best as it could. One of the assistant principals, a gregarious fellow and former football coach with a fog horn for a voice, resorted to a simple form of communication before technology invaded our lives. He simply stood in front of his office and shouted toward the various wings of the building to determine the status of the heating system in that area. However, one question caused quite a commotion all over the school. His main concern at the moment was the history wing located at the far end of the building. Unfortunately, he spotted one of the older female history teachers who had a reputation for being extremely straight laced and totally without a sense of humor. Without a thought as to how it might sound and using his best football coach's voice, he boomed the immortal words that lived on for years in the annals of the school, "Mrs. Jones, is it warm up your end yet?" The raucous laughter from all parts of the building was ample proof Mrs. Jones was not the only one who heard his question.

Front Porches and Fireplaces

The last several decades have seen massive changes in our society, some of them have been good and others have been not so good.   One obvious change that always surfaces in this conversation is the breakdown of the traditional family unit. If we accept that conclusion to be true, then we have to wonder what caused the breakdown to happen. Surely it wasn't caused by our society being deprived of the basics of life. This country, and our families included, has endured much hardship in certain times of our history and this has generally strengthened, not weakened, our family structure. As a matter of fact over the same period of time these changes have occurred our nation has experienced unprecedented growth and our lives have become much easier than those of our parents and grandparents. Certainly, advances in technology and medicine have made life more comfortable, for the most part. People are living longer, the environment is cleaner, our food supply is plentiful and safer, diseases that were once fatal can now be prevented or treated successfully and our automobiles are much safer and far more fuel efficient. Almost all of us will have to admit these have been positive changes for all of us. However, not all of the movement resulting from new technology has been in the right direction and certainly not all has been good for society as a whole. As a matter of fact, I would go so far as to say some have caused us to go backward in some aspects and have been very bad for our nation and for the world.   Albert Einstein once said many years ago something to the effect that, "It is obvious that our technology exceeds our humanity." This was long before the technology of today was even an idea in somebody's brain. The area, which has suffered the most, in my opinion, has been in relationships between people.

Technology has created a new generation of cave dwellers out of a large group of people, especially young people. Surrounded by huge flat screen televisions, computers, violent computer games, Smart Phones, I-Pads, Blackberries, and frozen pizzas, some folks never leave their house and have become socially inept.   They are actually more at ease and comfortable around their electronic devices than they are with other people. My wife and I attended an event at our local university a while back which included a lot of high school and college students in the audience. More than likely they were there only because their presence was mandatory for a class of some kind they were taking.   During the entire presentation, most of them were operating an electronic gizmo of some kind or sending and receiving text messages on their cell phones.   From our seats higher up and farther back, we could see the light from the devices glowing in their hands. It is not unusual to see groups of young people walking together but each one texting or talking to someone else on their phone. They are isolating themselves even in a crowd. We have placed so much emphasis on multitasking that the extremely important task of relating to others has been ignored. Interaction with other people is not considered important and this skill is fast disappearing.

I certainly do not advocate a return to the days when we had outhouses, party lines, carbon paper, manual typewriters, rub boards, and ice boxes.   However, it would be nice to see people get to know their neighbors, seal agreements with a handshake, gather with family around a table for meals and turn off their televisions when disagreeable and repugnant shows are the only viewing available. There is no law which dictates we have to sit in front of a television a certain number of hours per day regardless of the programming. How did we allow ourselves to get to this point as a society? How did we stray so far from a way of life that most everyone agrees was difficult in many aspects but also was kinder and gentler in many others? Why did we have to throw the baby out with the bath water?

My approach to most things can be described as simple, direct and free of abstractions. Sometimes I do not even let facts stand in my way. There are certainly instances when a simple answer to a complex problem is insufficient. However, there are also cases when we chase a complex answer which refuses to be caught when a simple one is stand right in front of us. I believe that the culprit causing many of our societal problems has been the absence of a front porch on our homes. Most of the houses built today have a space barely large enough to get the front door open without falling into the yard. Forget about having enough room for chairs and a porch swing for people to sit in and talk.   I have always lived in houses with a large front porch and a swing and, to me, a house without a front porch looks like it is missing a limb.   In days past, the porch was the place where the family gathered and talked. Sometimes major family decisions were made but generally the conversation was mostly about mundane things, but the key is that talking between family members took place. The discussion generally was about such things as the weather, work, gardens, school, weddings, church, births, politics, and funerals. People sitting around on their front porch attracted neighbors to walk over and join in on the conversation. Neighbors became our good friends, not just someone we waved at occasionally as we left our house. To this very day, my favorite place on warm nights is the swing on the front porch of our home. I am usually sitting by myself because my wife is a magnet for mosquitoes and prefers to stay inside. An occasional car passes on the road in the distance but there is little else to catch my attention. However, sitting outside on a dark, warm summer night is an auditory feast. Lightning bugs flitter across the yard and the frogs in the pond are a crescendo of chirping and croaking, the owls fly back and forth across the creek and locate each other by their strange, and sometimes scary, hoots and screeches. The call of the bobwhites is cheery, positive and uplifting while the whip-poor-wills have a mournful and sad sound. Sometimes a passing pack of coyotes or hounds chasing a raccoon across the creek bottom will get the dogs stirred up for a while but all of these things are typical and comforting sounds of the night. All of these put together create such a pleasant and enjoyable sensation that I sometimes catch myself wondering what I will do when age and circumstance take it all away. That is a concern I gladly postpone until another day.

Of course, some will say the real reason everyone gathered on the front porch was that it was far too hot to sit inside and this would be true. This is one instance where we can point our finger at technology that is wonderful in a lot of ways but, yet, seems to be responsible for causing our society to abandon one of the traits which allowed us to be better people. When air conditioners became affordable to the average family, the front porch soon became an added expense when building a house and virtually disappeared from the draftsmen's drawing boards. By placing a color television, cell phone and a computer with dozens of games in an air conditioned bedroom we have in a nutshell all the reasons most people no longer choose to sit outside in warm weather.

There was another feature of older homes that drew a family together in cold weather. Before modern heating systems assumed control of the temperature inside the house, homes were heated by either a fireplace or a wood or coal burning heater. Some homes have fireplaces today but they are either for decorative purposes or to supplement another type of heat. I am referring to those which served as the sole source of heat for an entire dwelling. The heat source in our old home was a coal burning, pot-bellied stove in the living room. Living in a house which was heated solely by burning something in a stove or fireplace is an experience most of us could have lived without but we will definitely never forget. My little narrow bed was located so that I could see the flames inside the stove through the damper, which allows air to circulate by moving it back and forth. More air meant a bigger flame and less air would smother the flame completely. Before he went to bed, Daddy would adjust the damper just enough to allow some air into the heater. This left two small openings only a few inches apart which, from my vantage point in a darkened house, looked exactly like the fiery eyes of a monster in our living room. Most nights were spent sleeping with my head under the cover. My daddy would get up before daylight and rebuild the fire, hopefully from hot coals which lasted overnight, and it had to be kept going all day. In our family that meant someone had to go out to the coal pile with a coal scuttle and bring in a sufficient amount to last a few hours. Needless to say, this responsibility always fell on the youngest in the family, which happened to be me. There were coal yards scattered all over town which delivered large chunks of coal and dumped the load as close to the house as possible. Some houses even had a chute which allowed the coal to be dumped directly into the basement if they had a furnace. Regardless, it took forever for a stove or fireplace to throw off enough heat to raise the room temperature just a few degrees. On cold nights, after supper, most families would gather around the fireplace or stove just to keep warm.   In this respect the fireplace or stove served the same purpose as the front porch, it brought the family together.

Unfortunately, the art of keeping warm in front of a stove or fireplace is fast disappearing and will soon be gone from our culture. If a person just sits without moving, one side becomes too hot and the other side is too cold. Some degree of experience is involved in knowing where to stand and when to turn to stay warm all over. Since it was too cold to stay in a room away from the fire, families gathered around close to the heat source and talked about the same topics as they did on the front porch. However, we eventually had to go to bed and that was another form of torture. Slipping into an ice cold bed and spending the night weighted down by a ton of quilts required to stay warm left a lot to be desired.

For several years after we were married, my wife and I lived in houses with only the heat from a wood burning fireplace to attempt the impossible; to heat the entire home.   I wore out four Poulans and I'm currently on my second Stihl. When some folks think of a fireplace they imagine romantic evenings with flames dancing across logs throwing out volumes of heat. Invariably, seated in front of the fireplace on a bear skin rug is a happy couple sipping on a cup of hot chocolate.   The opposite is actually true. Maintaining a fireplace is hard work and requires constantly looking after. In reality, what I think of is waking in the morning and dreading the long cold, shivering process of warming the house to at least one degree above freezing. Crawling out of a warm bed onto a cold floor and a freezing house every winter morning requires a constitution of steel and gets old very quickly.   I see my young children hovering around the fireplace eating their breakfast on the hearth while trying to fight off hypothermia. I recall countless hours spent cutting wood, hauling it to the house and stacking it outside as close to the house as possible. I remember covering the woodpile to keep the wood dry and I catch glimpses of myself sharpening saw chains so that the saw could cut through the logs. Building a fire every morning from hot coals banked the previous night was a chore no one relished.   Countless trips to the woodpile to bring in more logs for the fire in the cold and rain are not remembered fondly.   My wife complained constantly about the mess on the floor from bringing the wood in and taking the ashes out and dumping them.   On days when the chimney wouldn't draw correctly because of wind and rain, the house became very uncomfortable because the smoke would back up into the house instead of exiting out the chimney. A fireplace used as a heat source is a different creature than one used only on special occasions. The pop and crackle of a warm fire is a good memory but a lot of bad ones go into making it possible. So, those who insist the old ways of doing things are superior in every respect have a distorted sense of the way things really were.

Obviously, no one in their right mind would ever want to return to the days of no air conditioning and no central heating systems in our homes, work places and public buildings. It would be insane to believe this would make us better as a society. However, it does sadden me that some of the traditions and habits that some of us experienced as children have been rejected by today's world. I believe we see the results of this daily when the media reports on news events that seem common place today but were unheard of decades ago. To my outdated way of thinking, many of these problems could be avoided if people would just sit and talk to one another.   Surely, the results would be worth the effort. It seems we would all be better off if we kept what was good about the old ways and made every effort to blend it in with the new.   We have got to be smart enough to use all of our technology to the fullest extent but not allow it to gradually rob us of some of the good things that make up the backbone of any great nation; a strong family structure. What is happening to our families has the potential to cripple us as a nation.   It is even worse that it is taking place before our very eyes in the name of progress.

Growing Old Together

I first laid eyes on the girl who would eventually become my wife in 1962. We were both high school sophomores. I was being held hostage in a late afternoon study hall when Margo Wilson appeared as a transfer student from another high school. There was no instant spark, no love at first sight. If there was any connection at all it was a negative one because there were definite signs she didn't like me. For example, back in those days all county schools operated a school store which sold cokes, cookies, chips, and other items which are strictly forbidden by health conscious officials in schools of today. The revenue from the store was necessary to keep the doors of the school open. A store order was generally taken in study hall and one or two students would collect the store money and return with the goods and refund whatever change was due. The teachers always bestowed this privilege on students who were dependable and held in high esteem by the faculty. Possibly, another consideration was to select only students who could be trusted to be out of class unsupervised. This probably explains why I was never chosen. I felt Margo and her cohort always short-changed me in these transactions but the teacher did not like me and threatened to rescind my store privileges if I complained. I'm not sure but I think she had some sort of kick back deal with the teacher to help supplement her meager salary. Be that as it may, we found each other totally resistible and our paths would not cross again, except at a distance, for two more years. This was just as well for, at that time, my heart belonged to another. Her name was Faye and she sat directly in front of me in science class. She had long brown hair tied up in a ponytail, which completely mesmerized me. This was definitely a one-sided romance because a puzzling case of lockjaw kept me from expressing my feelings for her. Only later did experience teach me that for a relationship to have a chance to flourish, it must be two-sided. I knew many teenage boys who were suffering from the same affliction. However, exposure to teenagers for many years as a teacher and from observing my own two grandsons, it appears a major breakthrough must have been achieved while I was not paying attention and that dreaded disease has since been cured.

My future wife was born in Huntsville and lived in a single parent home with her mother for several years. As a child she was often shuttled, with her name pinned to her shirt, from Huntsville to Florence and back via Greyhound bus to visit her grandmother. It is strange how fate plays such an important role in our lives. Any number of things could have happened during these years and we would have never met.

One of my best buddies in high school was my friend Jerry. He transferred, with his family, from east Alabama when his father became a forest ranger in our county. We sort of bonded and were alike in many ways, but vastly different in one area. He was the kind of guy who had no problem getting a date and my weekends may as well been spent in a monastery. Our friendship was to play a key role in helping to overcome the strained relationship created by shady money handling by my future wife during study hall.

The social importance of the traditional junior/senior prom has lost a lot of glamour over the years. But in 1963, it was a very big deal. Our high school prom was to be held at the old VFW hall across the river. No luxury ballrooms, chauffeured limos, or exotic venues existed in this area at that time. A corsage and a white sport coat with white buck shoes were the only known requirements for boys. For girls it could have been different, but, what did I know? My plan for the night of the prom was to spend the evening at the Smokehouse pool room shooting pool by myself and eating the best burgers in this galaxy. If those burgers could have been franchised to a more socially acceptable outlet no one would have ever heard of McDonalds outside of the state of California. A few days before the event, my friend asked about my plans for the prom. He knew I had no plans and was on a mission I knew nothing about. Then in a roundabout sort of way he slips in the fact that Margo didn't have a date and maybe I should ask her. Now, remember, I knew Margo from the tenth grade and we had been like ships passing in the dark for the last two years. However, if I asked her to the prom it would give me the opportunity I needed to talk with her about all the money owed me from her trips to the school store. Many times in my life, I have ignored good, sound advice from a variety of people. My parents, brothers, teachers and pastors had offered me advice but my response had been to turn a deaf ear. Why this particular suggestion seemed worthwhile will never be known. It wasn't like my social calendar was full that night. It turned out to

Tom & Margo at their wedding in 1965. Maybe wearing white socks with a dark suit was fashionable in the 1960's.

be a major turning point in my life. To make a long story short, we went to the prom together and, as I write these words, have just celebrated our 47th anniversary.

Now, you may be telling yourself, isn't that sweet how that worked out all by itself? As veteran radio newsman Paul Harvey used to say, "Now, for page two." Many years later, at a class reunion, Jerry finally came clean. Margo knew Jerry and I were good friends and she was not reluctant to use our friendship to her advantage. She actually told Jerry to suggest to me to ask her to the prom.   The short time we had spent in study hall together in the ninth grade must have made a good impression on her. By the way, she convinced me I had not been short-changed in study hall. All in all, it was a good thing I could not speak to Faye in science class.

Forty-seven years later a much larger McDonald family has emerged. Rear, left to right, son Will, Margo, Tom, and daughter-in-law Kelly. Front, left to right, grandson Grant, daughter Amy, and grandson Reed. The little dog in Reed's lap is Ingram, namesake of Mark Ingram, former University of Alabama running back.

Outside of the gift of salvation, Margo has been the greatest gift God has ever given me. Not many people, including her mother, gave our union much of a chance. We have sort of grown old together. She has been my rock for a long, long, time. All along the way we have witnessed family and friends divorce, shattering many other lives in the process. We have never had her stuff and my stuff, her money and my money. We jokingly say, with a lot of truth, we are the dullest people east of the Mississippi River. This makes it extremely difficult to make and keep new friends. They soon move on to a better and more exciting group. We have even grown to like and dislike many of the same things, much to the annoyance of her family.

Without doubt, her adjustment to me has been much more difficult than mine to her. Her endurance is legendary among my friends and they can't believe we are still married.   A lasting marriage is not built on an expensive ceremony and writing love poems to each other.   If so, we would not have lasted six months. What both partners in a marriage are willing to do for their spouse is much more meaningful than volumes of pretty words.   Margo has been willing to do things to get us out of difficulties that would have sent many marriages down in flames. She has put my interests before hers on more occasions that I will ever know.   To my shame it took me far too long to realize that fact. For example, how many women, by herself, would lure a drunken three hundred pound boar hog out of a creek bottom with nothing but a bucket of shelled corn? The boar had gotten loose and became inebriated eating fermented apples off the ground.   What about loading a pickup truck with feeder pigs before daylight and hauling them to the pig sale in Russellville?   She must have spent considerable time talking with the other pig farmers because when she got home she had picked up smoking and chewing tobacco.   Incredibly, my wife avows to this day that having to deal with the pigs does not stand alone at the top of the list of embarrassing things she has endured for my benefit during our years of marriage. That honor belongs to a trip she was persuaded to make to a downtown drug store not long after we were married. A college course in the study of parasites had me convinced all southerners were riddled with parasitic worms which must be purged from our bodies. At my request, she bravely marched into the drug store and asked for a bottle of Aunt Jane's Vermifuge, which I understood, at the time, was a good remedy for worms. Apparently, the druggist was taken aback by her request which she had to repeat several times. Surprisingly, they happened to have a bottle on hand and, to the stares and snickers of the other customers, exited the store in disgrace with her purchase in hand. To my enduring shame, this sorry episode took place while I was sitting spinelessly in the car.

Thank you Lord for sending me a soul mate who has put up with me all these years, and who, almost always, still laughs at my foolish stories.

Is That All?

My wife and I were married one year after we graduated from high school in a ceremony so simple it was virtually painless. The only way it could have been any simpler was to go to the local court house and have the Probate Judge perform the ceremony. It cost so little that even Scrooge would have smiled. We were married in the living room of her home by my oldest brother Bill, who was a Methodist minister. I tried to pay him five dollars but he wouldn't take the money. He said something to the effect I would need it, and a lot more, later. The only flowers on hand were the ones my wife-to-be had purchased. As many as five or six pictures were taken with a Polaroid camera that developed its own black and white pictures in just a few minutes. The final product was about three inches by four inches, which was not quite suitable for framing. Years later when one of these pictures turned up in a cigar box I realized I was wearing white socks with a black suit. At that time in my life the word "faux pas" was not a part of my vocabulary and Miss Manners was nowhere to be found. I was a living, breathing example that ignorance is truly bliss and did not know it. Our honeymoon was a one night stay in the Holiday Inn in Decatur with a box of drive-thru Kentucky Fried Chicken from across the street. We were back at home the next day. I was in college and my new wife was working. It is real easy to be miserly when there are no pennies to pinch. When I hear others talk about the cost and planning required for a wedding ceremony today I experience something akin to a psychotic reaction. They are even bussing in livestock to take part in the ceremony. Not only do they cost mega thousands of dollars and consume most of a year to plan, the bride-to-be turns into something like a monster. This unfortunate turn of events leaves the groom-to-be with the impossible task of having to contend with two monsters, his future wife and her mother.

It was not long after saying our nuptials that Margo informed me she wanted only three things. Daydreaming was apparently not something she engaged in for long periods of time. I am also of the opinion her mother had counseled her to set the bar real low and not expect a lot. Anyway, her list consisted of a color television, a dishwasher and a trip to Hawaii. On a teacher's salary I was hoping she would settle for two out of three.

Let's cover these items in the order of their procurement. In the 1960's, color televisions were not all that common. The first television I actually laid my eyes on was in the late 50's and belonged to some relatives in Tennessee we always believed to be filthy rich. It was in a cabinet the size of a minivan and had a screen about one foot square. It made a constant sizzling sound like bacon frying and occasionally a shadowy figure could actually be seen, but not identified. It was not very impressive and I left fully content with our radio at home which was also the size of a minivan but had no screen but did have about five hundred knobs. It was obviously very heavy because it made our living room floor sag.   When color televisions became available in the late 60's my wife and I were finally able to purchase one on an easy payment plan. Remotes were not on the market then and it was necessary to physically get out of your chair and walk all the way to the television and manually turn it on or to change channels. This was a major reason that obesity did not rear its ugly head in America until remotes became available for every room of the house. However, not owning a remote was not a problem for us because we could only pick up one channel. When remotes did become readily available one of my aunts refused to walk between it and the television in fear of being zapped by the invisible rays it emitted.

The dishwasher wish was fulfilled a short time after we paid off the television. We were determined to limit the use of easy payment plans to one item at a time. The machine we purchased was not a built in model because a major revamping of our kitchen cabinets would have been necessary. Instead, we decided on the portable type which was rolled around to the sink when you needed to wash dishes. We used it for a dining room table when it was not washing dishes. Our experience with this type dishwasher would have made taking a chainsaw to the cabinets seem like child's play. Before it could be used, hoses were connected to the faucets and the drain was looped over into the sink basin. It was impossible to watch our new color television and use this machine at the same time because of the decibel level.   The noise generated by this machine was just a smidgen less than the sound from a Saturn V rocket headed on a lunar mission. Since it was not attached to any cabinetry, it had a tendency to sort of dance all around the kitchen.   This was not a problem until it was time for the water to be drained from the dishwasher into the sink, but was, instead, pumped onto the kitchen floor because the machine had danced farther than the drain hose could reach.   There was a bright side to this dilemma in that our floor was always spotlessly clean and required very little mopping on the days dishes weren't being washed.

This brings us to the final item on my wife's bucket list, the trip to Hawaii. This problem sort of solved itself when I was elected to a position with the state education association. Newly elected leaders were always sent to some glamorous destination to be trained for the arduous work ahead. However, I was soon to learn the only training I actually needed was how to pack my bag and occupy myself in an airline courtesy room waiting to fly away to another glamorous destination where we heard countless boring presentations about how important it was to spend all the dues dollars of our members. Otherwise, leaving money in the bank might cause them to get the idea their dues were too high and we were expendable. This budgeting process was handed down to us from our elected leaders in Washington. They may not have invented the idea but they had surely perfected it. I was willing to make this sacrifice and endure this grueling ordeal for over nine years.

As luck would have it, the training session I was scheduled to attend was in two of the Hawaiian Islands. Since all my expenses would be paid, my wife could tag along for little more than the cost of airfare.

We were to spend four days on the island of Kauai and then four more days in Honolulu on the island of Oahu. As most rednecks from Alabama would say, Hawaii is a nice place to visit but I wouldn't want to live there. We arrived in Honolulu and immediately took an island hopper to Kauai for the first half of our stay. It was dark by the time we arrived. Our room obviously overlooked the water because we could hear, but not see, the waves breaking on the beach. For some reason we were under the impression there were no mosquitoes or snakes in Hawaii. We were on the eighth floor of the hotel so we threw open the doors to the balcony and slept listening to the ocean sounds. The next morning we awoke to the fact that, not only are there mosquitoes on the island, but they can also fly really high. We were both covered in bites. But what's a few mosquito bites to someone from the South? Hopefully, they were right about the snakes but we took no chances.

It is common knowledge that when spending thousands of dollars to have meetings in places such as Hawaii one should not have to spend much time actually attending all those annoying meetings. We met for a couple of hours almost every morning and spent the remainder of the day taking in the sights of this beautiful island. The one thing my wife and I had looked forward to on this trip was not quite what we expected. The advance information we had received listed a Hawaiian luau as one of the night activities. Now, as mainlanders we think of beaches with a roasted pig on the spit and balmy Pacific breezes with ukulele music accompanied by hula dancers when we envision a luau. Margo and I had already donned our Hawaii flowery shirts and shorts when we were informed the event would be held indoors and dress would be more formal than casual. We were subjected to an event that only a group of teachers could over-think to the point that a pleasant experience turned sour. For some strange reason, they thought the atmosphere inside a community center eating barbecue and pineapple from plastic containers with piped in Gershwin music would be preferable to a real luau on a real beach. They were bad wrong and we were deeply disappointed.

It was a feeling of great accomplishment when I realized my wife's three wishes had become reality in just a few years. But, for all the fun we have had over the years telling this story, we soon came to the conclusion that "stuff" has nothing to do with the success of a marriage. If our marriage had been based solely on our ability to spend and accumulate things, we were doomed from the start. That is not to say that having more money along the way would not have been nice but it has not been the focal point of our marriage. We have been blessed far more than we could ever have hoped for and both of us know the source of all these blessings.

Beavers or Beepers

There is a lot said these days about being able to communicate, and conversely, failing to communicate, with other people. Books, talk shows, and magazines abound with experts pontificating on a topic which has been around for a long, long time and will probably always be discussed as long as men and women occupy the same planet. The truth is that most of us simply don't pay a whole lot of attention to what is going on and what others are saying. There is probably a lot of truth to the old adage that while others are talking we are not actually listening but simply thinking of what we are going to say as soon as they stop talking. However, there are a few times when an auditory filter comes in handy. A career in public education made a believer out of me. Every veteran teacher knows there are some things you will be better off not hearing, so it is simply tuned out. Walk the halls in any public high school today and you would never reach your destination if you stopped to react to every off-color remark that reached your sensitive ears.

Folks place a lot of emphasis on someone listening to them, and rightly so. Students want teachers to listen, teachers want students and administrators to listen, pastors want their congregation to listen, and those looking for a spouse want a significant other who will hang on their every word. However, couples who have been married a long time hear what we want to hear and sometimes we think we heard something that we did not hear at all. The older we get the more confused we seem to be about what the other one is trying to say. Women think men don't listen and vice-versa. It actually works both ways and sometimes at the same time. It other words, neither party is tuned in to what is being said. My wife and I are good examples of this phenomenon. A while back we were riding to work together while my truck was in the shop for repairs. It was early and my wife is not much to carry on a conversation in the morning. She has to sort of ease into the day gradually while I am wide awake when my feet hit the floor. If I ever have a good idea, it is early in the morning. Any discussion regarding any kind of idea in the morning would be irksome to my wife. If I discovered early in the morning I had won the lottery I would be hesitant to inform my wife until after lunch.

On this day we had ridden several miles in total silence, as we often do, and suddenly something came to mind I had wanted to tell her the night before but had forgotten. A colleague at work had the opportunity to travel to the Smoky Mountains with her husband on business and asked me to recommend a good place for them to eat. That area is our favorite part of the world and she knew we visited there as often as possible. I had told my friend at work of a place in Pigeon Forge, Tennessee that we really liked. It is a wonderful restaurant bordered by a picturesque stream, an excellent view of the mountains and really good food. Upon returning to work, she told me they did not get to go there but actually visited another restaurant which offered a unique way for guests to respond to the proverbial dinner bell. When there was no available seating, the patrons were given beepers and told to enjoy the local shops and they would be summoned electronically when a table became available.   The device would emit a beeping sound which is technical speak for, "Let's eat." Now, here comes the part about miscommunication. First, you have to remember it was very early and my wife was operating on autopilot. Second, you have to remember, and this is very critical, that each time I said "beeper", my wife actually thought I was saying "beaver." Conversely, each time my wife said "beaver", I thought she was saying "beeper." This conversation began with me telling her that my friend and her husband went to a new place in Pigeon Forge that gave them a beeper (beaver to my wife) to carry so they would know when their table was ready. Not quite believing what she thought she had heard, she responded, "Gave them a what?" Rather innocently I answered, "A beeper (beaver)." Her interest level jumped several notches as the fog of sleep began to disappear from her brain. She said, "Why would they give them a beaver?" Not believing she could not understand the purpose of a beeper, I patiently explained. "They gave everyone waiting for a table one to carry with them so they wouldn't have to stand in line and wait. They walked around the shopping area and the beeper told them when it was time to return to the restaurant."

102

Her confusion growing by leaps and bounds, she asked the only logical question, "How would the beaver know anything about their table being ready?" My knowledge in this area is very limited and I apparently knew even less about what I thought my wife was hearing. I replied, "I guess it just buzzed or something. But what I don't understand is how far from the restaurant you could walk and the signal to the beeper still be able to reach you." "So you are telling me the beaver receives some kind of a signal from the people in the restaurant," she countered. I came back with, "Absolutely, otherwise the beeper would never know when to buzz." Bent on getting to the bottom of this ridiculous tale, my wife was warming to the task at hand, "Where did they get all those beavers?" Electronics is not exactly my cup of tea, but, like husbands tend to do, I gave it my best shot. "I don't know, probably from some supply store but I bet they are actually Japanese. They get them in bulk and are probably cheaper." Recognizing another good stupid husband story to amuse her cohorts at work, she dug deeper, "Where do they keep the beavers while they're walking around waiting for their table?" To me the answer to that question was very obvious, "The women probably put them in their purse or maybe strap them to their belt. I would just put one in my pocket so I could tell when it buzzed. I don't know much about beepers but I think you can make if vibrate if you don't want it to make the buzzing noise. It's very annoying to be in a place where a lot of people have beavers buzzing in their pocket." In an attempt to summarize the incredible tale she had just heard, she said, "You are actually telling me there are people walking around Pigeon Forge with Japanese beavers in their purse, or pocket, which buzz, or vibrate, when their table is ready at the restaurant?" Defending my honor, I passed the buck by replying, "That's what Charlotte told me and I am just telling you what she said." In a last attempt to wrestle some sanity from this bizarre beginning of another day, she asked, "Where do they put these beavers while they're not being used and when the restaurant is closed? I imagine they would require a lot of looking after." Not understanding her concern for a lot of circuit boards, I responded, "Probably locked up somewhere to keep them from being stolen. I bet a lot of people try to hang on to theirs and not return it." With a final sigh of exasperation, she turned and focused on the road. The sooner she could get me to work the sooner her world could recoup some sanity. We lapsed into a period of silence with each wondering what in the world had just happened.

In due time this preposterous conversation was straightened out and the magnitude of our miscommunication became apparent. I guess the moral would be, never believe everything you think you are hearing and expect the same from others.

Promises We Make

Most of us are taught to keep our word. When we make a promise it is important that we do what we said we were going to do. At least in times past, it was important to most everyone to be considered a person of 'their word.' Major deals were made with a handshake and wars were fought for the sake of honor. All of us have, at some time, made a promise to God. I have made many such promises. Some of my promises were made during spiritual highs when God's presence was very real and very personal. However, most were made during times of stress, medical or family emergencies, or when I felt trapped with nowhere else to turn. An old saying goes there are no atheists in foxholes and sometimes we find ourselves in a foxhole during our normal, everyday lives. We beseech God to come to our rescue and deliver us from bad situations. When our worst fears do not materialize we shrug off any commitments we may have made under duress and pretend it never happened. It is an understatement to say that promises are easier to make than they are to keep.

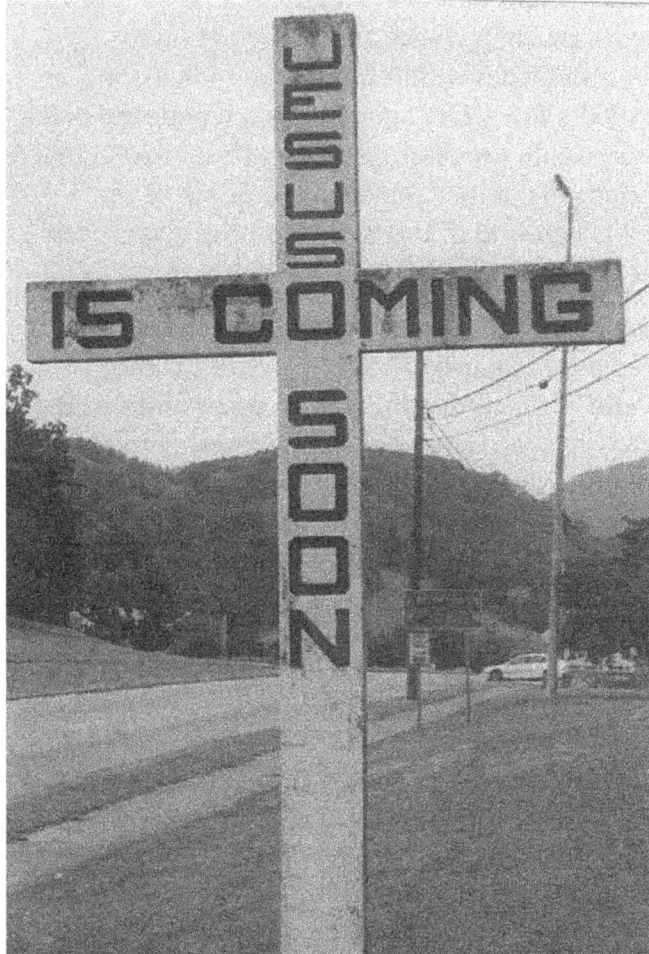

If you have driven the roads of the South you have seen some of the crosses erected by Harrison Mayes.

A while back, my wife and I visited the Museum of Appalachia in Clinton, Tennessee, a few miles north of Knoxville. Several years ago, a fellow by the name of John Rice Irwin realized the rich and irreplaceable history of the Appalachian region of this country was being lost to urban sprawl and development. He realized the simple tools and everyday items he remembered from his youth were being tossed aside and their practical use forgotten. He fought against this by collecting items that told the story of how this area was settled and how the people survived in this rugged, but beautiful part of the world. It was his goal to make others aware of the ingenuity and toughness demonstrated by these mountain folk as the frontier disappeared to the west and left them cut off from civilization on their remote mountain tops and deep in the isolated valleys. He attended auctions and struck up friendships with mountain folks who sold or gave him items for his collection. His rich assortment of folk artifacts became a museum in 1969 and has a worldwide reputation as the crown jewel of anything relating to Appalachia. All of the items in his museum came from within a 200 mile radius of his home and he continued collecting until he died a few years ago. This is a wonderful place to visit if you love the mountains and the way of life that was necessary to survive in that difficult environment. There are literally thousands of items on display. Some of the displays have a printed story that gives the background of the item and how it was used. A one-day visit will not do justice to all that is there.

As we approached a rather large display of items, I was instantly aware that I had seen some of these things before. Scattered around were dozens of crosses, some standing and some lying on the ground. Some were made of wood, some of metal and others of concrete. Then I realized these crosses were a regular sight alongside roads I had traveled throughout my life. All of them had the words, "Jesus Saves," or "Get Right with God," written or embedded on them. Even though these crosses were very common, at least in the Southeast, I had never thought about how, or why, or who, had placed them there.

Harrison Mayes was a miner in the coal-rich Appalachian region for many years. One day, deep within the ground, a mine collapse found him trapped with no way out. In a pitch black tomb, with his life very much in danger, he made a promise to God. He said he would serve God all the days of his life if God would only let him live and go back to his family. Miraculously, and I don't know how, he was able to get out safely. Instead of forgetting his promise, as I have done many times, he set about doing what he vowed to God he would do. At the time, the only thing that came to mind was to take a young steer he owned and use that animal to help send his message. He painted the words, "Jesus Saves" on both sides of the steer and turned him loose to roam the community. He then began to make small wooden crosses with similar messages and placed them along roads in his community. As time allowed, he moved farther and farther from home and marked the location of every cross on a roadmap. He saved a few dollars from each payday to buy materials and gradually moved from wood to metal to concrete. Eventually, he was able to purchase an old tow truck to help erect the large, concrete crosses weighing hundreds of pounds. The remainder of his life was spent fulfilling his part of the promise he had made to God on that fateful day in the mine. He erected some 1600 signs during his lifetime and even had plans to place signs on the moon and Mars. In addition to the signs, he thought of other ingenuous ways to carry out his promise. One such way was to use whiskey bottles, which he considered a vessel of sin, to spread the message of salvation far and wide. He placed a note in these bottles and tossed them into the mountain streams near his home. There was the possibility these bottles were carried from tributaries of the Tennessee River into the main river, on into the Ohio and then the Mississippi. From there their passage to the Gulf of Mexico and the oceans of the world was not impossible. After his death, all his leftover materials lay neglected until his family donated them to the museum and his story was told by John Rice Irwin.

This wonderful story of how one man kept his promise to God makes me ashamed when I remember how my promises have been swallowed up by things so minor I cannot even recall. God has been faithful to me all the days of my life, in every situation, without fail. A part of one of my favorite songs at church goes,

"Oh no, you never let go, through the calm and through the storm. Oh no, you never let go, through the highs and through the lows. Oh no, you never let go of me."

Even though I have been perfectly willing to let go of God, he has never let go of me. The sad truth is that my faithfulness to him has been based on convenience. The story of men such as Harrison Mayes should serve as an inspiration to all of us who have ever made a promise to God.

East Florence Playgrounds

It doesn't take a real observant person to realize the countryside is chock full of places for kids to play. Ignoring the highly recognizable Disney, Six Flags and Dollywood mega playgrounds which are within driving distance, and also quite expensive, there are countless opportunities close by. There are waterslides, putt-putt golf courses, paved areas for basketball and tennis, swimming pools, fenced areas set aside with swings and slides with rubberized material covering the ground to soften those inevitable falls, church owned family centers, soccer fields, softball and baseball fields and probably many others that fail to come to mind. Yet, many of today's kids will quickly tell you there is nothing to do around here.

Growing up as a kid in the 1950's was a different world as far as organized recreation was concerned, especially if you grew up in East Florence. There was no television to speak of and certainly no computer games to occupy our time so we were forced to be creative and make do with what was available. The only playground actually labeled as such in the community was located at the corner of what is now Huntsville Road and Minnehaha Street. An area we once considered to be the equivalent of Yankee Stadium is now totally consumed by a Salvation Army church building and grounds. But, when I was just a kid we lived only a hop, skip and jump across Sweetwater Creek and this was ground zero for sandlot football and baseball games. All we had to do was go down the hill to the creek, walk across the footbridge and down the street and we were there. The Florence Recreation Department sponsored only four youth football teams in the whole city. The East Florence White team practiced on the playground until it disbanded in the late 1950's. Boys who lived in East Florence and wanted to play were forced to go to Weeden School and play on the Blue team. The other teams were the Reds and the Yellows, one of which was at Patton School and the other in North Florence. The old playground had very little actual equipment but a lot of open space. A shallow, round wading pool for small children that, to my knowledge, never held a drop of water was located across from the knitting mill on Minnehaha. A wicked spinning contraption called a flying jenny was also part of the equipment but was prone to injure those who cranked it up fast enough to overcome the Law of Gravity. It eventually reached a speed where you were not able to hold on any longer and your body went flying off the machine. It was not really kid friendly and child safety laws of today would shut it down immediately. The best piece of play equipment was the really nice set of swings located on the side of the field nearest Minnehaha Street. They were made of metal and long chains connected the seats to the overhead bar. The long chains allowed the swing to achieve amazing altitude if the one in the swing was so inclined. It was the only piece of equipment on the playground that actually worked as intended.

The backstop for baseball games was in the corner of the field where Minnehaha Street veers off from Huntsville Road. The area immediately behind the backstop was covered with weeds and vines which made it extremely difficult to find a ball fouled over the backstop. The balls we played with were actually covered with black electrician's tape because the cover had disappeared long ago. The tape was not very durable and there was always a piece fluttering in the breeze when it was thrown or hit causing considerable fluctuations in speed and direction. Our only solution was to just keep adding more tape as needed. We went through more tape in a summer than most electricians did in a lifetime. Once, while we were searching for a lost ball, a man pulled his car over in the church parking lot across the street and just watched us for several minutes as we continued our search. Eventually, he reached inside his car and pulled out a small box which held a brand new white Rawlings baseball. He tossed it across the street onto the field where it rolled for a few feet and then just sat like a precious gem. Not sure of what to make of this unusual event, we initially just stood and stared at the ball until he said it was ours. This news triggered a stampede and we converged on the ball like hungry wolves chasing a rabbit. When we looked up to thank him, he was gone. Playing with a new, slick leather baseball, after years of balls covered with black tape, was a new

The author's own playground, his backyard, with his dog, Blackie.

experience for all of us and our skill level immediately jumped up several notches, or so we thought. Maybe, watching us play ball and constantly searching for the only one we had brought back some memories from his boyhood and he knew all about black tape.

The playground described above was the only official one and comes immediately to mind when someone refers to a playground in East Florence. However, the kids living in the vicinity knew of other places to play depending on what kind of play we had in mind. Very close to this playground were two other areas which were very attractive to kids but provided ample nightmare material for mothers. A small feeder stream meandered from

110

nearby "Railroad Hollow" on its way to the creek. A large warehouse building had been built squarely in its path but the architects wisely left sort of a tunnel under the building to accommodate the stream. It provided a nice, dark place to play with multiple hiding spots and it had its own running water. This was a prime play area in that it led directly to a small railroad trestle which brought box cars into the back of the warehouse to be unloaded. Following the track a little further brought you to the much larger trestle which crossed Sweetwater Creek. A great amount of caution was necessary to play on this trestle because to be caught in the middle by an approaching train left only one choice, jump the fifteen or so feet into the creek below. If you had a lot of time on your hands, this spur line connected to the main line only a few hundred feet away and the main line could be followed all the way to the long, high trestle which crossed over the Tennessee River. Although I am sure some did, none of us ever had the courage to walk that trestle. Some of the guys would always act like they were thinking about it but we always just turned around and made the long walk back to East Florence.

The greatest place for us to play closest to our house was what we called the gravel pit. The land on the corner of Livingston Street and St. Paul Street had been used as a source of gravel for roads long before I was born. Years of excavation left a very large and deep pit before the site was finally abandoned. This old gravel pit was used as a playground by generations of kids in the area. It was also a convenient place for drunks and lovers to pull into late at night and be totally out of sight to anyone passing. The main attraction of this place was the almost vertical walls, which we climbed like monkeys. Several attempts were made to dig a cave at the base of one of these walls but none ever got more than a few feet into the bank before we decided digging a cave was too much like work. No one was ever actually killed while playing in the gravel pit but my brother, Bobby, came real close. Pretending to fly was a really big thing with boys back then and my brothers took it way too seriously. One of our older brothers, Joe, convinced Bobby that if he tied cardboard wings onto his arms and flapped them fast enough he could actually fly. What better launching pad than to hurl oneself off a high cliff? Adequate cardboard was secured from one of the warehouses close by and the project began to take shape. It almost came to a tragic end when Bobby backed away from the edge and, with his cardboard wings strapped on, ran as fast as he could and leaped off the edge of the forty foot cliff. Fortunately, he landed in the top of a tree at the bottom and escaped his brush with death with only major bruises and lacerations. It would be an understatement to say that our daddy was not amused. However, he had to be more than a little embarrassed that two of his sons could be that stupid. My brother's attempt at non-mechanized flight became almost legendary in the community. As long as my older brothers were alive and started talking about their days growing up, this topic always headed the list. Several generations of boys tried to make the flat area inside the pit into a baseball field but the rocks were far too numerous and we never succeeded. Today, the area seems to be mostly overgrown with trees and weeds and has become a dumping ground.   Maybe all the kids are out playing tennis or soccer.

The area on the far side of Sweetwater Creek from our house was known simply as the "woods." It seemed like a giant forest but, in reality, it was probably less than fifty acres. Regardless of its size, it was a great place for a bunch of boys to play. We climbed trees, swung on vines, played cowboys and Indians and, in warm weather, topped it all off by going for a swim in the creek. More than simply a place to play, it gave us a refuge from the world of adults who were always calling us away from what we were doing to ask us what we were doing. It was important then and it is important today that kids have as much time as possible to just be kids. That idea seems to be a novel concept to a lot of parents.

The days of the childhood we thought would never end did indeed come to an end. It is impossible to pinpoint exactly when that time occurred but that is probably the way it should be. If we knew exactly what was actually happening in real time we would never let go and that would not be normal. The world has changed so drastically since then sometimes I feel I lived on another planet as a boy, and maybe I did.   The people I knew in East Florence have, long ago, become memories and the places are no longer recognizable or have disappeared completely.   I have thought many times of taking my grandsons back there and showing them all the marvelous places I knew as a boy but that kind of thing hardly ever works as planned. An author named Thomas Wolfe said in so many words that we can't go back home again and experience proves he was right. Sure, we can return to the physical location of our home but that is not what he meant. The deeper meaning is that we can never recapture our past no matter how much we wish we could. As children we generally have such strong emotional attachments to our home that, once severed, can never be rebuilt. So much would be lost in trying to translate those days across three generations that my grandsons would never comprehend or appreciate my feelings about what I was trying to say.   In other words, you would have to have been there to understand.

County Fair

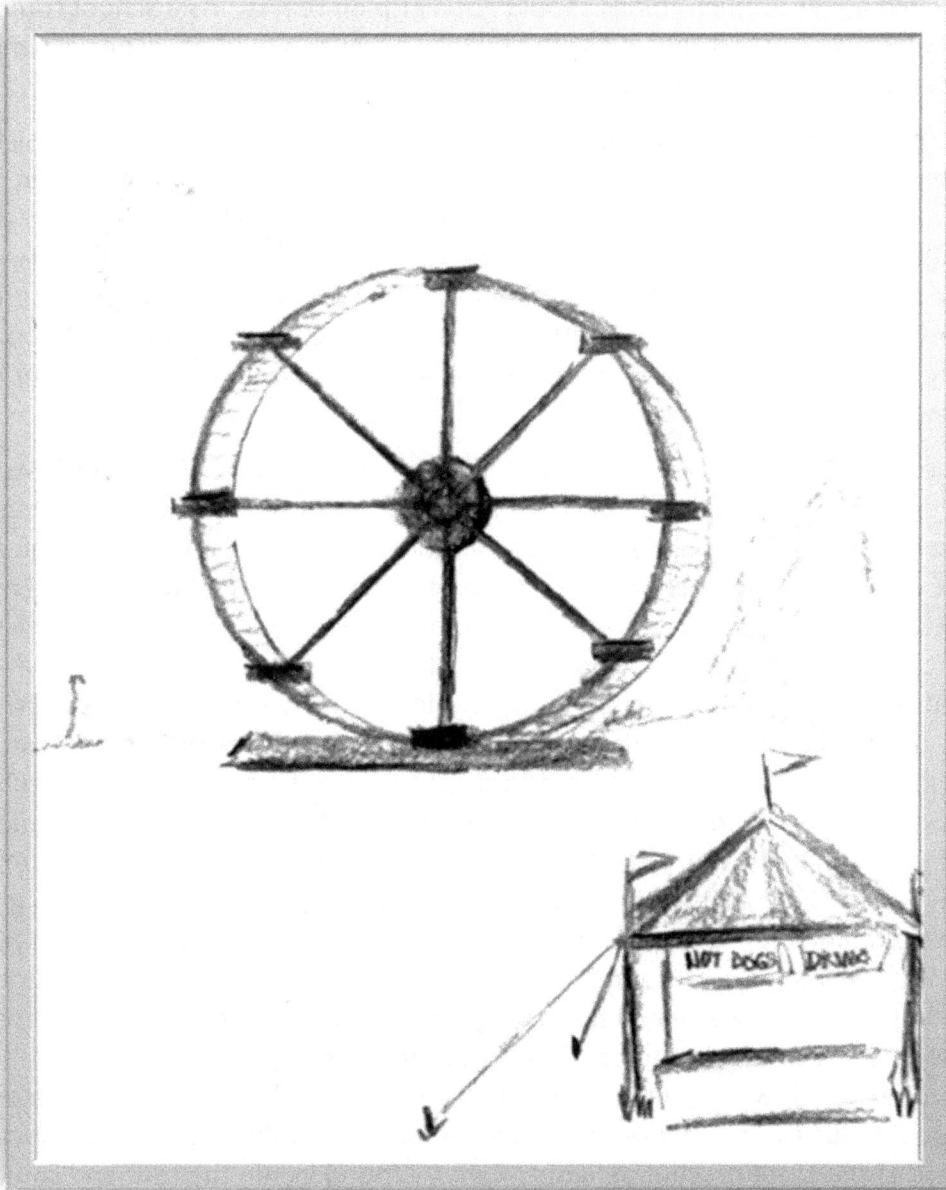

There comes a time in the life of most young people, especially boys, that they ignore what they have been taught and do things and go places they shouldn't go. Most of us have been guilty of this at some time while growing up. Parents who believe their children would never do such things should get a grip on reality. As a school counselor for many years I was always astonished at the lengths parents would go, especially mothers, to deny their child was guilty of an offense of some kind at school.

My parents raised six boys and one girl which was not an easy task. They had great expectations for their children and expected us not to act like we had been "brought up in a barn." One of my favorites was when my mother admonished me not to act like a little "heathen." She also used that word to describe all of my "heathen" friends. Much later in life I learned that a heathen is defined as an "uncivilized person." She sure hit the nail on the head about my friends. With most of us, many times the expectations of our parents are forgotten in the fog of the moment as we try on our wings and experience the thrill of newly found independence.

One thing my father did allow his children to do was to drive without a license. Hindsight probably taught him this was not a good idea but this was before our society became so litigious. The practice of driving without a license was fairly common at the time but it was still against the law. So, at the age of fifteen, my father allowed me to drive my 1952 Studebaker to the county fair, accompanied only by my equally naïve friend, who was also only fifteen. The fair was a big deal back in those days. We anticipated going to the fair as a child today would look forward to going to a Disney attraction. A scarcity of entertainment often made the fair the only show in town. That night, my friend and I had nothing in mind except to go to the fair, enjoy some rides, eat burgers and fries, and try to win a prize playing some of the rigged games. We didn't know it at the time, but it was probably easier to beat the odds and win the lottery than it was to win a teddy bear at the fair. Nevertheless, after paying our fifty cents to get in at the gate we embarked on an experience that was beyond anything we could imagine at the time. We started looking around the midway for the right place to begin our night at the fair. Unfortunately, we picked the wrong place to start. Directly in front of us, and deliberately located off the beaten path, was a tent some might politely call, a 'gentleman's club'. However, it was really a strip show. We happened to arrive on the scene when the out-front guy, the barker, called forth a couple of the 'performers' to give the gawkers a little taste of what delights might be found inside the tent and could be purchased with only a couple of dollars. It was, deliberately, a very brief, but enticing, performance. Most of the guys gathered around the tent looked like they had been caught stealing candy. They were shuffling around, looking down at the ground, and

114

glancing over their shoulders. Apparently, they came with their mothers. The barker said it was now time to separate the men from the boys and a significant portion of the crowd melted away down the fairway, as we should have done. However, my friend and I, not knowing any better and operating strictly on the ignorance of youth, lined up to pay our two bucks. Actually, we did know better, but we had the confidence only teenage boys and dictators can have. We believed the worst case scenario would be for the man taking up the money to tell us to get lost, and fully expected that to happen, and send us on our way. There is no doubt that adequate laws are on the books specifically to protect fifteen year olds, like us, from this very kind of activity. However, most fifteen year olds are not famous for having good sense and we were no different. It was not like we were burly, mature for our age, and shaving on a regular basis. We were fresh-faced, slightly built boys barely out of puberty. I guess every law ever passed has been broken at one time or another so we forged ahead. The man simply looked at us, concluded we were at least twenty-one years of age, took our money, and ushered us into the tent of iniquity. If we wanted to go that route we could say it was not our fault they let us in and blame them for not checking our age. Come to think of it, that would be a perfectly acceptable excuse in today's world. Inside the tent, the décor was rather primitive, consisting of a few wooden benches and a sawdust floor. However, there was no need for fancy furnishings because, as far as I could tell, there were no interior decorators in the crowd. There could have been a dead skunk on the floor and no one in this crowd would have noticed. Shortly, a few scantily clad women paraded across the front of the tent, did a couple of moves that proved beyond a doubt they never had dance lessons, and disappeared out the other side. The performance could barely be described as being bawdy. Today, women wearing far less are commonplace on beaches, magazines and even television. A Victoria's Secret catalogue would put them to shame. But, remember, this was 1962, and we were only fifteen years old. At the time we believed the show was over and we had gotten our money's worth. As we turned to leave, it was announced a far better viewing could be had inside the next tent if we were only willing to cough up another couple of dollars. What the heck, we had come this far, why not go one step farther? We were not the first or the last to be led astray by this flawed logic. Suspecting another con, we lined up with our money in hand and prepared to enter the inner sanctum. Again, our age seemingly made no difference. The décor was the same but it was a far different show. On what passed for a stage, we noticed what appeared to be a large, closed up oyster shell. Music played, the lights went out and a spotlight, of sorts, illuminated the oyster shell. It began to open, very slowly, and a woman emerged. There was a popular song in the sixties about a stripper with the name 'Little Egypt.' She purportedly concluded her act wearing nothing but a 'button and a bow.' I have been told it is very important, when writing, to use the appropriate word when describing an event so I must be careful here. It has been said there is a difference between "naked" and "nekked". One becomes naked when undressing to take a shower. Slithering out of an oyster shell in a tent at the county fair with no clothes on, in my opinion, is an appropriate use of the term "nekked." This lady apparently forgot both her button and her bow. While the word bawdy did not describe what we saw in the first tent, it definitely was an understatement for what we were seeing in the second tent. After a few moments of stunned silence, I began to hear what reminded me of the jungle sounds so familiar to those of us who grew up watching Tarzan movies. There were hoots, whistles, screeches and grunts coming from somewhere. Actually, these noises were coming from some of the guys in the audience. Being a complete novice at this type of thing, I was wondering if the correct protocol was to make these type sounds. However, it didn't matter, as I was unable to make any type sound at the moment. The remainder of her act would be hard to describe since our eyes were so bugged out of our heads that we were not able to see clearly. The performance could have lasted two minutes or two hours, it was impossible to say with any degree of certainty. It was a good while before we were able to even talk. The show eventually ended and we stumbled out a back entrance and shuffled back to the midway.

The remainder of our night at the fair was rather bland and uneventful from that point. The oyster lady experience had left me virtually penniless and without sufficient funds to even attempt to win a teddy bear or ride the roller coaster. Our night at the fair was over practically before it had begun. Despite all the bravado that kind of experience produces in a teen age boy, I knew my parents would be ashamed of me. My daddy always told his kids he would trust us as long as we didn't give him a reason not to. The knowledge that I had betrayed that trust produced a guilty feeling that far exceeded any other that I might have felt that night.

Cars

The cars of my youth are vastly different from today's vehicles. Automobiles of the 50's and 60's were easily recognizable simply by their body style. Most of today's cars look like jelly beans with doors. Yesterday's cars were rather simple and easier for ordinary folks to do simple maintenance chores. Many American youths grew up fiddling around with old jalopies. I have read that one major factor in the success of the United States in WWII was that when an American tank, jeep, troop carrier or other motorized vehicle broke down the troops around it simply fixed it using know how gained from growing up around family cars and farm vehicles. On the other hand, German vehicles were abandoned where they sat when they developed a problem and were lost to the war effort. The youth of Germany had not grown up tinkering with automobiles as had their American adversaries. Today, it would be fool hardy for anyone like me to even attempt something very simple on a car. The computerization of every system on board has made it very difficult on shade tree mechanics. The computer on one of these cars cannot be adjusted with a crescent wrench. Many of the car parts familiar to most of us cannot be located and some are no longer necessary. Parts such as the starter or generator were easily recognized but today it is almost impossible to find the dip stick to check the oil level. A fairly simple task such as replacing the spark plugs is now impossible for the average person.

After our marriage, my wife and I could not afford anything remotely dependable. We bought and drove what we could afford. Yards full of abandoned cars proved many other families had the same problem. However, like a lot of men, I tried to do what I could to save money, but had only little success with a lot of debacles mixed in.

One such disaster occurred when I attempted to paint an old VW Beetle. The original paint job had disappeared under a coating of rust so anything would be an improvement, or so I thought. Since I owned a spray gun and an air compressor, it didn't seem to be too big a deal. My workshop had two large doors on the front which would open wide enough to get the car inside. However, once inside, there was not enough space to close the doors but I forged ahead. I knew it was important to keep paint from drifting and covering the entire shop so I had to build something like a paint booth around the car. Clear plastic sheets I hung from the ceiling failed to totally solve my problem. The plastic did not quite reach the floor so I extended it by taping pieces of our local newspaper to the bottom, all around the makeshift booth. After hours of taping and sanding, I was finally ready to paint the car. The driver's side door was a good place to begin, so I started spraying and slowly made my way around the entire bug before I stopped. My paint supply ran out just as I finished. Standing back to inspect my work, a major malfunction was evident. Apparently, a breeze came through the open doors and blew the newspaper taped to the bottom of the plastic against the bottom of the driver's side door. Since the paint had not totally dried, it peeled off without tearing. But, the newspaper left a calling card. The ink had transferred to the wet paint on the door. As a result, now printed upside down at the bottom of the door was a perfect replica of the paper's name and the day's top headline. It was no use to wipe the area and paint it again because I had no more paint to cover the resulting smear. For the next several years, I drove the car the way it was, much to the amusement of friends, colleagues and students where I worked. The Auto Body instructor at our technical school offered to fix it but it was a one of a kind paint job and I declined. When we later traded the old VW, I told the salesman it was that way when I bought it.

Another do it yourself calamity took place when we owned a Rambler station wagon. The Rambler was built by American Motors and was quite economical to drive during the gasoline crisis of the 1970's. We had owned the car a couple of years when it suddenly became impossible to start when it was raining or foggy. Otherwise, it started without a problem. This proved to be very inconvenient and annoying. A friend suggested a thorough check of the distributor cap to see if it was cracked. A tiny, hairline crack was indeed visible in the cap. A crack in the cover would allow moisture to seep into the distributor, wetting the points, thus causing the engine not to start until it dried out. A new distributor cap could be purchased for about thirty dollars but that was a lot of money to us, about one third of my weekly salary. The auto parts guy suggested spraying the cap with a coat of clear sealer which would stop the moisture in its tracks. At home, I removed the cap, carefully tagging all the plug wires, and gave it a liberal coating on the outside. One of my many flaws is that I am prone to go overboard on simple tasks and do not leave well enough alone. So, to be absolutely sure the problem was solved, I went ahead and sprayed the inside of the cap. This was a very big mistake and it created an entirely new problem. When one attempted to start the engine, a small explosion took place inside the distributor cap, blowing it cleanly off the distributor to which it was attached. This, too, proved to be an inconvenience, especially to my wife since she was the principal driver of the car. The explanation was quite simple. The sealer coat I foolishly sprayed on the inside of the cap contained a combustible material which slowly released a volatile gas, thus trapping it inside the cap. Turning the ignition created a spark and ignited the gas, resulting in the explosion. Constantly having to raise the hood and replace the cap grew to be very embarrassing and caused some strain in our relationship. My wife is a very smart woman and after several dozen small explosions suggested a new distributor cap would probably be a wise investment. Good advice is hard to come by and should never be ignored.

Olden Times

It seems every generation lays claim to all the best memories in life and relegates later generations to whatever good times they can conjure up. Of course the good times remembered by the younger crowd never seem to quite measure up to the way it used to be in the minds of the older folks. Things change regardless of what we would like to see remain the same. Indians, or Native Americans today, used to have a saying that "only rocks last forever." Now we know that not to be exactly true after we study how the Colorado River created the Grand Canyon. But, I do lament the fact that many things that were such a big part of growing up in my generation seem to be denied to younger folks.

My grandsons will never feel the excitement growing in late summer as we began the long wait for the county fair. It was such a big deal that all the schools turned out early so that students would have a chance to go. We saved money for weeks to be able go on all the rides. We sold drink bottles, scrap iron and even picked cotton on Saturdays to have enough money for late September, when the fair finally came to town. Kids privileged enough to have visited Disneyworld would scoff at something as trivial as the county fair.

In the backyard of the home place in East Florence. Front, left to right, Tommy and Johnny. Rear, left to right, Bobby and Virginia.

My grandsons will probably never experience swimming in ice cold, spring fed creeks during the hot, unbearable dog days of August. As a teenager, we frequently relieved some farmer of his excess watermelons after dark and sat around our swimming hole and ate only the sweet hearts out of every melon. This was after skinny dipping and running around like savages until

120

we were exhausted. I was blessed to be able to saddle up my horse and ride all day across unfenced fields, woods, and narrow dirt roads that are now clustered with houses. I owned a large, white gelding that would stand patiently in the middle of Cypress Creek while I used his back as a diving platform and then stand unattended for hours until it was time to go home. He faithfully carried me for untold hours riding back and forth past the home of a girl I thought I was in love with, although she didn't know it at the time. It was my fervent hope she would come outside and ask to ride with me. That sort of ending occurs only in fairy tales and all those trips were in vain. However, it does point out some of the illogical thought patterns of a fifteen year old boy and explains some of the predicaments we create for ourselves. This girl sat directly in front of me in science class and her long ponytail brushed across my desk when she turned her head. At a class reunion some forty odd years later, I finally had the nerve to tell her about my high school crush on her. She was quite surprised.

Our current society will not allow my grandsons the freedom to load up an old truck and go to Panther Creek and spend days fishing and loafing on gravel bars, totally unsupervised, eating nothing but Moon Pies and burned wieners. We built fires from driftwood to ward off the snakes and lay for hours watching the lights of strings of barges churn their way up and down the mighty Tennessee River. Where they were going or where they came from, we had no idea but often pondered this question. My grandsons will also never get to experience how we purchased and paid for items in the old general stores in our community. Now days, one has to produce all sorts of ID in order to buy something without cash. As a teacher, I was paid only once a month, therefore I never had any ready cash. No problem. We had a charge account at the community stores and when we bought gas, groceries, or my kids bought a soft drink, we simply told the owner, "put that down." He would take his ledger book and write the date, item purchased and the price. Our daughter came home from college to visit one weekend and brought her friend from California. The friend thought our daughter was stealing when she left without paying for her items. When payday finally arrived, at months end, we would go in and settle up. This kind of credit is not obtained by filling out a bunch of papers and submitting to a background check. It was available because the merchants knew us and knew our word was our bond. It was a much simpler, and more pleasant, way to conduct business. But, those days are long gone. Too much meanness has made a casualty of trust at this level.

Another thing the younger folks seem to be missing out on is the old clunkers we drove around in. Of course, it was kind of unusual for a teenager to have a car in the late fifties and early sixties. Those of us who were fortunate enough to have one usually inherited it from an older brother. Somehow, the guy with a car always wound up with a surplus of friends. When I was teaching, especially during the 1980's and 90's, it was amazing to compare the vehicles in the students' parking lot with those in the teachers' parking lot. The students' cars were invariable newer, sleeker, and more expensive. My first car was a 1952 Studebaker, inherited from my brother. Initially, I thought I could run with the wind but, to my dismay, I frequently had to put it in reverse and back up steep hills, much to the amusement of my free loading friends. The motor was too weak to pull the car up the hill. My dad was a smart man. The old Studebaker was also lacking a workable heater, which made it very uncomfortable in cold weather. This problem was somewhat alleviated by purchasing cans of Sterno from the local military surplus store. This product is immediately recognizable to hunters and campers. It consists of a flammable gel in a container about the size of a Vienna sausage can which burns slowly and sends out considerable heat. With several cans of Sterno ablaze inside the car and little puffs of smoke coming from the cracks in the windows, from behind it probably looked like the car was on fire. The cans are used quite a bit today under serving trays to keep the food warm. However, I am quite positive the manufacturer does not recommend their product for use in a moving vehicle, but we were desperate and OSHA was not yet born. Next in line was a 1955 Chevy, also inherited from my brother after he wrecked it and joined the Air Force. I drove it for years without a hood, muffler or fenders. The first cars I actually helped pay for was a 1957 Chevrolet and a 1964 Ford Mustang. With the exception of the Studebaker, the others are now considered classics and are very valuable. It is a pity that only hindsight is 20/20.

The author's first car was a 1952 Studebaker with a heater that wouldn't work.

It is a known fact that every generation firmly believes that every succeeding generation has had it easy all their lives. It is difficult, if not impossible, to convince them that life, as they remember it, was not all snow, ice, and working in the fields all day long. For example, my sister had told her children for years how she, her brothers and friends, had to walk five miles to school every day. Tired of hearing this tale, one of her sons loaded her into his car one day and took her back to our old home place and told her to point out the exact route she had to walk to school. When they reached the old school site, it was less than one mile from our house. The only thing that proved was that the world is shrinking.

Up On the Roof

My wife's retirement came a few years after mine. She was a stay at home mom until our children started school, and consequently, was a few years behind in building retirement credit. As a result, I was left to my own devices at home. She was uncomfortable with this arrangement because she knew, from experience, how I frequently became ensnared in circumstances beyond my control. Most of my humiliating experiences have been self-inflicted and she felt her physical presence would be a soothing balm, so to speak, and be a deterrent to some of the bad decisions I tend to make when she is not around.

My workshop is located on a hill above our house and is my pride and joy. In fact, I spend so much time there it is, at least partly, responsible for our marriage lasting almost fifty years. All the time spent in my shop gives meaning to the belief that absence does, indeed, make the heart grow fonder. One day, of course my wife was at work, the first chore on my list was to climb onto the shop roof and patch a leak in the attached shed. It was to be a very short, simple task taking only a few minutes. While propping my ladder against the building, I took note of a rather stiff breeze. After reaching the top and taking a few steps, I wish I had taken further note when the breeze blew my ladder over, leaving me stranded on the roof. I quickly realized I had a problem when I heard the sickening sound of the ladder sliding along the metal roof and clanging to the ground. It was not a good feeling. After carefully analyzing my situation, I considered my options. The first option was to just sit and wait about five hours for my wife to come home from work. This was completely unacceptable. Not only would it be an agonizing wait, but it also involved a great deal of humiliation. The joy she would experience in driving up and seeing me trapped on the roof was something I could not bear. I would never be able to live it down. She would delight in repeating the story at every opportunity to friends and family for years to come. In addition, she would use it as further evidence to support her contention that I could not be trusted to stay at home by myself. The second option was to jump off the roof at its lowest point. Of course dropping ten feet to the ground in a free fall was very dangerous. A broken leg or ankle was at the bottom of my list of things to accomplish on that day. I concluded that sitting on the ground with a broken leg waiting for my wife would take the exact same amount of time as it would while sitting on the roof waiting for her without a broken leg. That is not even taking into account the pain factor. Common sense dictated I could not jump directly from the roof to the ground.

There simply had to be another way out of my predicament. Further study of the situation was necessary. The area around the front of my shop is free of trees. However, the rear of the building almost touches a wooded area. The closest tree was an oak sapling only a few inches in diameter. My eyeball test placed it to be about six feet from the roof. My only hope to avoid years of grief was to leap from the roof to the sapling and climb down. That was the best case scenario but, at best, the plan was fraught with opportunities for disaster. To be successful, agility, speed, courage and strength would be necessary. Unfortunately, not one of these traits was in my rather limited set of physical skills.   However, I had seen many movies at the ten cent Saturday matinees where my boyhood heroes, Roy Rogers and The Lone Ranger, escaped from far worse challenges without breaking a sweat. On the other hand, the Three Stooges were also on my hero list and they always failed the simplest of tasks while looking ridiculous and sustaining serious injuries. My mind was made up.   I would attempt the acrobatic jump in order to get out of my predicament. My foolish pride would not allow me to wait for my wife to rescue me.   My dilemma was similar to a wild animal that chews off its own leg while caught in a steel trap. I would do anything to escape. I gauged the chasm between the roof and the tree. Like an Olympic broad jumper, I backed up an appropriate distance and began my sprint toward the take-off point. The comparison to an Olympic athlete ends here in that I was dressed in overalls, sweat shirt, work boots and a John Deere cap. There was no tight, sleek, stream-lined body suit for me. I passed the point of no return and realized there was no turning back. The rate of speed at which I left the roof would be the critical difference between a successful jump and an extended stay in the hospital. My take off was good, actually, much better than anticipated. Unfortunately, the sapling was even less substantial than originally thought. I hit it with a great deal of velocity and the tree immediately bent backward under the force of my momentum. Getting a good hold on the tree proved to be much more difficult than I had planned. It seemed to be consciously avoiding my grasp but I managed to hang on until it snapped back into an upright position. That little amount of stability allowed the law of gravity to kick in and I slid gratefully to the ground, much like a fireman on a pole. Victory was mine when my feet touched the ground.   So what if I had tree bark and pieces of limb imbedded in my face? When my wife arrived home later and asked how my day had gone, I replied, "It just seemed to fly by."

Sorry About That

My family is well aware that I am technologically challenged. This unfortunate affliction places me at a severe disadvantage when attempting to carry on an intelligent conversation with any person possessing even a scintilla of knowledge in the field. I do not remember having this exact problem when I was younger and it could perhaps be a by-product of growing older. There is no doubt that the aging process does indeed cause one to do certain things differently and even to do other things that cannot be explained except by the gray hair that was brown years ago. One thing that baffles me is that I cannot for the life of me remember to turn off my blinker light after completing a turn. Now, my truck is supposed to be programmed to do that for me but it is not always dependable. It seems that my left blinker light has been turned on since 1992, or close to it.

It is not that I do not enjoy the convenience of technology it is more along the lines that I do not trust it as is the case with my turn signal. This is not the only instance where supposedly fail safe technology has turned against me. I have an abundance of evidence that the GPS system in my truck has led me astray numerous times. Our laptop computer senses my negative vibes and malfunctions constantly while I am using it but performs flawlessly for my wife. My cell phone refuses to release to me the messages the screen clearly states await me. In spite of this our society has become increasingly technology dependent and that is very frightening. A fellow told me the other day he had tried to get the oil changed in his truck that very morning and the dealership could not do it because the computer was down. Where are we as a supposedly advanced society when an automobile mechanic cannot change the oil in a vehicle without the aid of a computer?

As I said, I do enjoy the convenience technology brings to my life. One of my favorites is the keyless entry to a vehicle. My first experience with this marvelous advancement was several years ago when I purchased a used Chevy pickup. Much to my surprise, it had a keyless entry and I soon grew quite fond of it. Unlocking a door manually is not a big problem, but to unlock the door from fifty feet away gave me a feeling of superiority over those pitiful commoners wrestling with an armful of packages and trying to insert a key into the door lock. I must admit I also got a kick out of startling my wife by pressing the alarm button when she walked by and the horn started blowing. However, after a few years of use, it became unreliable and finally quit. A trip to the dealership cost me sixty bucks for a service visit and a battery and about three more days of use and it quit again. The price of a new unit was, in my opinion, exorbitant, so, I reverted to the tried and true method of using the key but never gave up on once again experiencing the happiness I enjoyed with a keyless entry system that functioned properly. Several months later, at a dealership across the river, I decided to get a second opinion. It was significantly less expensive than the previous quote so I drove away with a brand new entry system.

The issue of trust soon reared its ugly head and I was always fearful it was not going to work. This paranoia that technology is out to get me is not confined to my keyless entry. The same sick feeling descends upon me when I am around remotes, credit card readers, children playing games on a computer and pay at the pump gas stations. This contraption found around banks and other businesses which doles out money is a complete mystery to me. My children and grandchildren ridicule me but I can't help it. Because of this mistrust, I got into the habit of talking to the new keyless remote and warning it of dire consequences if it ever failed me. I even called it names which shouldn't be repeated in public. Not long afterwards, coming out of my doctor's office in town, I headed toward what I thought was my truck, with my keyless unit in hand. From several feet away, I began pressing the unlock button, but the truck lights were not coming on, indicating it was not unlocking the door. Closer and closer I walked and it was still not working. All my fears had come true because I knew it would eventually let me down. As I reached the driver's side door, I said in a menacing voice while looking down at the remote in my hand, "Unlock that #$%$#@%$# door right now you sorry &%$#@*$." It is entirely possible that I used some other inappropriate words which I immediately regretted. As my gaze shifted to the door of the truck, I looked up into the terror filled eyes of an elderly lady sitting behind the steering wheel of what was probably her truck, but it definitely was not mine. It was the same color, make and model but, I noticed a little too late, had a different type tool box. While waiting patiently in the parking lot for her friend or loved one to come out of the doctor's office she had absolutely every reason to think she was being accosted by some foul-mouthed thug who planned to take her nice truck. An immediate apology was certainly in order but that would have given her more time to summon the authorities. There is no doubt I would have apologized at a later date if it would have persuaded the presiding judge to lessen my sentence. The first thing to come to my mind was to run. The second thing that came to mind was the difficulty I would have, if she managed to overcome her fear and call 911, trying to explain to my wife why I had been arrested at the doctor's office. I could visualize being examined by the court appointed psychologist, during my thirty day court mandated confinement in the mental health ward. There was no way I would be able to convince anyone, especially the authorities, I was simply talking to my keyless entry and had no intention of harming the lady and taking her truck. That, in itself, was ample reason for the court to order a complete mental evaluation. So, I did what any red-blooded American male would do in a similar situation. I scampered away like a yellow dog. A fast exit from the parking lot took me safely out of any immediate danger of apprehension. Normally, I don't go through Lawrenceburg, Tennessee, in order to get to my home in Cloverdale but I thought this might be a smart move to out-flank any roadblocks. Not long after that incident, I traded trucks and began searching for a different doctor.

Swimming Holes and Boys

Boys and swimming holes go together. It's hard to decide which came first, kind of like the chicken or the egg. A bunch of boys will make a swimming hole out of a stretch of water snapping turtles and cottonmouths won't go near. During my growing up years considerable time was spent around creeks and swimming holes. There is a lot to be said about the value of being able, as a boy, to spend a day walking along a creek bank, being still and watching things that happen without getting involved. This goes a long way towards helping to understand there are creatures other than ourselves in this world. Watching the bass and brim pop the insects on the surface of the water and looking for the almost invisible pike lying up against the bank waiting for a meal to come along are memories never to be forgotten. The excitement of seeing the tell-tale wake of a swimming snake break the smoothness of the water and the plop-plop of the snapping turtles as they drop from logs into the water upon your approach makes a boy appreciate some of the inner workings of nature. The stillness of such moments leaves a mark inside you that lasts forever. For proof, ask a group of old men and if their memory is good enough they will mention such things and their eyes will grow teary.

Contrast the stillness of a silent walk along the creek bank to the raucous chatter and laughter of boys in a swimming hole. My first encounter with such a place was in a little creek that meandered in the bottom below our family home. Only a stone's throw away from our house, it was like a treasure in our back yard. The creek was small by anybody's standards but for a small boy experiencing his first foray away from the peering eyes of parents, it was a grand adventure. I am convinced these short moments of independence, as fleeting as they are, add up and make total independence less difficult as an adult. The little creek had to be dammed up with rocks and limbs to make enough deep water to learn to swim. A shelf of bare rock covered by only a few inches of water had grown so slick over the years generations of boys knew it as Slippery Rock. The older boys, including my brothers, were lucky to escape serious injury when they dove from the high limb on the old hackberry tree on the other side of the creek. Given the chance, boys will show out at the risk of life and limb. But, that is what boys do and generations of mothers hope their sons live to become men and not show up as a statistic.

A swimming hole on a much grander scale was available after we moved out of town to the country. The Knothole drew boys from miles around and had as much appeal as a modern day waterpark. To reach this gem of a swimming hole one had to park at the end of a dead end dirt road and walk maybe a half mile across scrubby pasture land and a snaky creek bottom. Of course, there was always the temptation to drive down by unlatching Mr. Jim's barb wire fence gap and braving mud holes and tree limbs to reach the creek bank. This was most often done at night when one had several ripe, heavy watermelons snatched from the tempting patches of unsuspecting farmers. However, they didn't remain unsuspecting for very long and these night time forays were often met with shotguns and trip wires. That terrifying experience only made them taste sweeter.

The creek was ice cold with swift water running out on one end. Impatient spring time swimmers would emerge from the water with blue lips and goose bumps the size of marbles and proclaim the water to be fine. A small slough on the far side had just enough weeds to make snake encounters very much a reality. A mud pit had been scooped out close to the trail on its way to the creek. It was always wise to be cautious when approaching this area because there was always the possibility an ambush was ahead with mud balls serving as the weapon of choice. Those being ambushed often fled in panic through a bit of flora we called itch weed, which was an understatement. Bare legs would be set ablaze by running through this vile weed and the only antidote was time and cold water.

The first swimmers of the day wisely tossed a few large rocks into the water before offering their bodies to the teeth, or fangs, of whatever was lurking below the surface. Every boy knew the presence of snake doctors on the water was a sign that at least one of their name-sake was surely present. The deepest part of the swimming hole was maybe eight to nine feet most of the summer. The real attraction was a cable hanging from a large tree which, if brave enough, would carry you far out over the creek with sufficient altitude to cannonball anyone foolish enough to swim within your range. Of course, to accomplish this feat, it was necessary to launch yourself from the highest part of the platform and time your release perfectly. It was always wise to go ahead and drop because the return trip was fraught with danger of a different kind in the form of a sudden stop against an unyielding obstacle, the platform. The effectiveness of the swing was made possible because of the old wooden platform that had to be rebuilt almost every year, having been swept away by winter's floods. Four of Mr. Jim's sturdy saplings, some old barn wood, nails and a hammer and teenage ingenuity always solved this problem. Our biggest fear came to fruition one year when the early arrivals discovered the cable had broken and lay covered with mud and gravel in the shallow water of the creek. A legend was born that day in May when a kid with the nickname "Chicken" stepped forward and offered to climb the tree and repair the swing. Prior to this day he had never distinguished himself in any way. He was short, nondescript and easily overlooked. Apparently Chicken had no fear of heights and his reputation as not being real smart was enhanced on this particular day. He obviously had no fear of death either because the forty foot fall surely would have been the end of him. We held our collective breath as Chicken inched up the tree and onto the limb out over the water. He called for the cable as a surgeon would call for his scalpel. It wasn't clear which worried us the most, our hero of the moment being killed or injured, or spending the summer with no swing. Thankfully, the only thing that died that day was his nickname. He made it without falling and his legend lives on to this day in the hearts and minds of those of us who still cherish Knothole memories.

Swimming holes are as therapeutic to a boy as psychiatric help is to a neurotic. Cares and worries are washed downstream with the water and disappear around the far bend. The chance to be a boy is an opportunity that comes along only once in a lifetime. When it escapes, it is gone forever. Coincidence or not, my wife and I built our first home on the creek only a few hundred yards upstream from the old swimming hole. My friends asked frequently about the Knothole and did I ever go there? For some reason I visited it only once in the twenty years we lived so close to it. The dead end gravel road had been paved and had become door to door houses. Mr. Jim's fence and the wild plum trees had disappeared and became part of somebody's yard. The mud bank our feet had kept clear of grass for so many years had grown up in weeds. Gravel had almost filled in the swimming area and the old platform was nowhere to be found. The hands that so willingly rebuilt it every year were no longer available for that kind of work. The old swing was still there, hanging by a thread. I don't know what I expected to find on my visit, certainly not my boyhood. What I missed most were the voices. There was no shouting, no laughter and no mud ball battles being fought. Those boyhood voices now belonged to men scattered in homes in far places with jobs, families and not enough time for even a quick plunge in a cold creek. Distance and time cause the bonds of boyhood to be stretched to the point of breaking but I don't think they ever actually break. I know this to be true because when I drive past a creek full of boys it all comes back and I remember once again the days I thought would last forever.

The Last Switchback

The only overnight accommodation in the Great Smoky Mountains National Park, other than campsites, sits atop Mt. LeConte, which rises some 6593 feet above sea level. However, spending the night in the rustic lodge atop this majestic mountain overlooking Gatlinburg is no easy task. The only way to reach the top is by foot. If you wish to go to the top of nearby Clingmans Dome, for example, you could ride to the top of the second highest peak east of the Mississippi in the air condition luxury of a vehicle of your choice, be it motor home or automobile. A short hike up a paved walk will take you to the highest point in the Smoky Mountain Range, 6643 feet, some fifty feet taller than LeConte. It is a tradition for LeConte visitors to pick up a stone at the bottom of the mountain and take it to the top. A sizable rock pile sits at the very top and it is hoped, by LeConte enthusiasts, that eventually the size of the rock pile will exceed the fifty feet needed to make it taller than Clingmans Dome. It appeared to be about thirty feet short of the record when I added my stone to the pile.

A trip to the top of LeConte requires you to take one of several hiking trails of varying degrees of difficulty. The most popular, and shortest of these trails, is probably the Alum Cave Trail but there are several others. LeConte Lodge is such a popular destination those wishing to spend the night must make reservations about one year in advance, unless you wish to sleep in the bear proof cage on the trail a few hundred yards short of the lodge. When one thinks of a lodge so popular that reservations are made a year in advance, generally a plush resort with pool, hot tubs, great roaring fireplaces, five star restaurants and many other guest comforts come to mind. The lodge atop the mountain has none of the amenities we normally associate with a lodge. There are several rustic cabins but none have water or restroom facilities. Each cabin is equipped with several double beds. Depending on the size of the group booked for the night, it is entirely possible to share a bed with a complete stranger. Primitive public restrooms are located close to the lodge but they seem a long way off in the middle of the night. Within the last few years a flush toilet has replaced the latrine-like facility that was in place for a long time. A dining hall offers wonderful meals in great quantity for those with lodge reservations. However, coat and tie are not required. Instead, the patrons are generally wearing hiking boots and clothes made somewhat rank from the long climb. Supplies to the lodge come by Llama train up one of the hiking trails. Mules were used for many years but their large, hard hooves did more trail damage than the cloven-footed Llama.

A while back I traveled with a group to spend the night at the lodge. What should have been a six hour hike turned into eight hours because of rainy weather which made the trail hazardous. A hike up any mountain is generally a challenge. Our trip to the top began with the Appalachian Trail for a few miles and then the Boulevard Trail the remainder of the way. Anyone who has hiked any distance on the AT will quickly tell you that rocks and roots are real hazards. Some short sections of the trail are narrow ledges along rock faces with anchored cables to hold to. The worst things about hiking up a mountain are the switchbacks which seem to go on forever. Just as you think you can see the mountain top and your burning legs and lungs are going to get some relief, a switchback takes you in the opposite direction and the sky disappears behind a tunnel of trees and bushes. I have developed a theory of sorts which applies to those who hike in mountainous terrain. We shall call it Tom's Theorem on Vanishing Goodwill. A group beginning a hike up a mountain all start out with a great deal of goodwill toward everything and everybody. Optimism is rampant. Every little wildflower along the trail, every bird call, every bit of flora is interesting and invites a great deal of discussion. It is difficult to move more than a few steps without someone in the group exclaiming and gushing over a new find or sound. However, as the

Tom McDonald hiking up a switchback on the Appalachian Trail in the Great Smokey Mountain National Park.

ascent grows more difficult, less and less time is spent dawdling and more time is spent sucking air into your lungs and trying to remain upright on quivering legs. Frivolous comments by one's companions are easily ignored and sometimes met with hostile stares. What was once a merry band seeking adventure has now become dispirited and almost venomous. Hence my theorem; trailside goodwill vanishes in direct proportion to the difficulty of the ascent and corresponding increase in altitude. Time spent on the trail must also be factored in as a multiplier which will exacerbate the rancor factor.

I have noticed that many hymns we sing in church compare life to climbing a mountain and it is a valid comparison. Whether we are very young and just starting out in

135

life or an adult at the base of a high mountain ready to begin a climb, one thing is certain. That certainty is we don't know what we are about to get into and some difficult times lie ahead. If we stood at the base of a high mountain and could see clearly every switchback we had to encounter on the way to the top, we might be inclined to give up before we ever started. But, if we give up before we begin, we miss all the beauty along the way and at the top.

The same is true for life. For every flower we smell and every bird call we marvel at along the way, life seems to throw another switchback in our path. Occasionally, we may even encounter a rattlesnake or bear smack in the middle of the trail we are taking. Life is indeed full of switchbacks but sometimes we have to propel ourselves upward by grabbing onto roots and saplings and inching ahead the best we can under the circumstances. Life is not a sprint to the finish and neither is hiking up a mountain. It is not a destination to reach but it is a journey. We have to stop and catch our breath along the way.   There is no better way to catch our breath than to ask our Creator for help.

One of the great joys on the way up a mountain is to find a good spot, sit down and simply enjoy being there. In life, as in mountain hiking, if we look in only one direction we see only switchbacks and more difficulty. If we look in another direction we see vistas that cannot be described with simple words. We see God's creation at its grandest. Hiking up a mountain eventually brings one to the last switchback which will carry you right to the top. In life we will eventually reach the very last switchback and we are faced with looking out over an eternity that never ends.   Maybe God is easier to see from the top of a high mountain but we will never know until we conquer that last switchback.

Fighters and Floggers

Growing up when and where I did there were chickens all around me. My grandfather, whom we called Papa Lindsey, lived a short distance away and he had a huge hillside fenced in for his chickens. He grew White Leghorns and sold eggs for income. We dined on the hens that did not produce eggs according to his standards and, fortunately for us, he had high standards. Papa frequently summoned me to come and help him catch a possum when it got inside his pen. Most critters, like a fox or bobcat, will catch a chicken and take it elsewhere for a leisurely meal. A possum will kill as many chickens as it can catch in one night and leave them scattered all over the pen like feather pillows. Apparently, they are not smart enough to flee the scene of the crime and are generally still hanging around the next morning. There was never any doubt of the culprit's identity when a possum was involved.

Papa's son, my uncle Carlos, lived on a hill above us and was a notorious grower, trader and fighter of game roosters. He also was notorious for drinking and sometimes disappeared for days at a time when he was off fighting chickens. Much later in life I found out that my uncle Carlos, or Bill as his friends called him, was a highly decorated soldier and among the first American G. I.'s to cross from France into Germany after the Allied invasion in WWII. It may have been he was drowning some mighty bad memories in a sea of whiskey. My brother Bobby apparently fell under the influence of our uncle Carlos and soon became involved in raising and fighting game roosters. This was something he did as long as he was able

The author's brother, Bobby, enjoyed roosters so much his wife lovingly had one engraved on the back of his grave marker.

and loved chickens until the day he died.   As a matter of fact, his wife loved him enough to have a game rooster engraved on his tombstone.

For those not in the know, a game rooster is as proud and haughty as any creature God put on this planet. Their colorful feathers, especially their tail feathers, make them a beautiful bird. Many people raise them to show but they are also raised to fight.   A game rooster will fight its reflection in a mirror until it is too exhausted to stand. They can't be turned loose with other roosters or they will fight until there is only one bird standing. Without question, rooster fighting is bloody and brutal. It is against the law to fight them, as it should be. Over the years, people have engaged in such blood sports as dog fighting, bear baiting and coon-on-the-log events, apparently for amusement. There is also a lot of gambling, and drinking that keeps such activities alive in spite of being unlawful. Someone once asked President Lincoln how he felt about rooster fighting and he responded something to the effect that if we allow men to get into a ring and try to kill each other we shouldn't deny roosters the same privilege.

My first flock of chickens came when my dad brought home a dozen or so day old chicks someone had given him.   I guess I was hooked on chickens from that point on, not to mention the genetic connection.   However, my interest never gravitated over to the fighting side like it did with my uncle and my brother and so many others in our little community. I built a pen and constructed a small chicken house out of scrap lumber from my dad's workshop. As long as we lived there, I had a flock of chickens. They were a mixture of breeds. Some were slackers from my grandfather's flock, some were rejects from my uncle or brother and some I traded for myself. My favorites were the Rhode Island Reds and Dominiques.   One of the Dominiques was a huge rooster raised from a chick. His name was Rocky but had never shown any aggressiveness or willingness to fight.   A friend of mine offered to buy him for a dollar. Now, I was quite fond of Rocky but a chance to make a quick dollar didn't come along every day for a kid back then. He wanted my rooster to give his game roosters some practice before actually putting them in the ring to fight. It was a common practice to buy cheap roosters in order to train their birds. Most of the time, the sparring partners didn't last long. Much to everyone's surprise, Rocky killed his fighting bird very quickly. In fact, he killed or cowed every bird he went up against. A cowed bird is one which runs away and will not fight and winds up in the stew pot.   Rocky actually had a good career as a fighter before being retired to stud, so to speak. Apparently he was one of a kind because his progeny didn't fare so well in the ring and his genetic line died quietly in a huge, steaming pot of chicken and dumplings.

It was recently brought to my attention that some people keep chickens as pets and allow them to live in their homes. This is astonishing because chickens leave behind a lot more than feathers and mites.   Furthermore, it is my staunch opinion that chickens are too dumb to be house broken. In fact, I believe chickens are dumber than any other critter I have ever been around for any length of time. This includes dogs, cats, pigs, cattle, horses and donkeys. This lack of intelligence apparently does not automatically prevent them from being good companions in some people's estimation, but it does in mine.

An even greater problem is that not all chickens are friendly toward people. My rooster, named Kramer, was a prime example of such a fowl. He was a Black Australorp and a sleek, fine looking bird. The hatchery catalog describes this breed as good for both egg and meat production and, goes even further to state: they generally are good natured. If this is the case, then Kramer's gene pool had suffered a serious mutation. For some reason, he did not want me in his presence. There was no reason for his hostility toward me as he was never mistreated. As a matter of fact, he was fed all he wanted to eat, allowed to live in a dry chicken house and provided with a harem of hens. In spite of all this, Kramer could not disguise what he really was, a flogging rooster. Papa Lindsey warned me from early on that there was nothing worse than a flogging rooster and Kramer proved him right. Chicken people are familiar with flogging roosters and can actually predict an impending assault by observing their behavior. Initially, the bird will sort of hop up to you sideways with his head tilted toward you and a wild look in his eye. Also, the feathers on his neck are extended. At some point, he will launch himself at you with wings flapping and spurs extended. It is a very unnerving experience, especially for little children and those who tend to be wary around chickens. It takes a lot of experience to learn to stand your ground against such a bird. Kramer showed signs of being a flogger soon after maturity. The first-dust ups were minor but he grew bolder as he gained experience in the art of flogging. He would actually run to the chicken house from the far reaches of the pen to get a crack at me. Every time I went to feed and gather eggs, he was always there. A swift kick launched him out the door on several occasions but he was persistent. Our very volatile history came to an end one day when I cracked him across the head with a stick I always carried to defend myself against his attacks. He collapsed like a sack of rocks and appeared to be dead. He finally opened one eye and I could tell it was kind of glassy looking.   When he started to regain consciousness he tried to shake off the blow and attacked again before his head fully cleared and he had regained what little sense he had.   Maybe he was seeing two or three of me because he missed the real me and crashed at a high rate of speed headlong into the oak wall of the chicken house, knocking himself out for the second time in a matter of a couple of minutes.   I believe Kramer's erratic behavior proved beyond a shadow of a doubt my long held belief that chickens are not real smart. Apparently a rooster's skull is not padded enough to withstand multiple concussions. Kramer never recovered from the second blow to his head and slipped silently to the other side. Even though his demise was at his own hands, it was just as well because pay back was coming. Revenge is never appropriate when it involves people. However, it is condoned when it involves flogging roosters.

Surplus Roosters and Raccoons

It seems highly unusual, but the last few years have caught me with a surplus of roosters and raccoons around the house. Most of my backward friends advised me to just shoot all of them and be done with the problem. That seemed rather harsh so I was left to my own imagination to devise a more humane method. Both problems involved a different approach but did share a common destination where they would all live happily ever after, or so I hoped. There is no claim on my part that this method is perfect or without risk. However, desperation is the mother of creativity, or something like that.

Let's begin with roosters and some background information. Chickens have been a part of my life since childhood. I grew up sort of surrounded by chickens and this carried over into my life as an adult. Therefore, I think I know a little about chickens although I don't claim to be an expert. It is common knowledge that hens lay eggs to reproduce, not just so we can enjoy eggs in their various forms for breakfast. Without the presence of a rooster, their eggs are not fertile and will never produce a baby chick. On the other hand, a rooster in the chicken pen doing what comes naturally allows the hen to lay a fertile egg. If this egg is incubated properly, for approximately twenty-one days, a newborn chick will emerge. Incubation can involve a man-made device called, appropriately, an incubator, or the hen can sit on the eggs with her body heat serving the same purpose as the incubator. By the way, a setting hen is notoriously ill-tempered and one should act accordingly when in their presence.

Nevertheless, all knowledgeable chicken people know that when eggs hatch, approximately half will be males and the other half will be females. If several hens are allowed to set and hatch little ones this law of probability will quickly produce an excessive number of roosters. Hens are much more valuable because they provide eggs for the family table. On the other hand, roosters are a problem. They eat just as much as a hen but provide nothing in return unless it is decided to put the rooster on the table in the form of fried chicken, or even chicken and dumplings. This creates an additional set of problems, especially if you are squeamish. In order to get it to the table, the rooster has to be dispatched, or terminated. I have done this many times by simply wringing their neck, as taught me by my grandfather. The other method is to chop off their head, which should be self-explanatory. However, more detailed information may be necessary to explain the practice of wringing a chicken's neck. It basically involves grasping the chicken tightly just beneath the head and swinging the body in a circular motion until it separates from the neck, which you are left holding in your hand. When the carcass hits the ground it frequently runs around without a head. This spectacle can continue for several minutes and young children tend to be frightened and should be quarantined until the chicken finally gives it up. Hence the phrase, "running around like a chicken with its head cut off". Believe me, this is a technique involving some skill and a strong stomach. Anyway, after the rooster is dispatched, using whatever method you may choose comes the equally unpleasant task of plucking, or removing, the feathers and gutting the bird. Disposal of these leftover parts can be a problem. It is readily apparent that the long road from the chicken pen to the frying pan is much messier than going to the grocery store and purchasing a nice, clean package of chicken parts. Another negative is that a rooster raised in the barnyard provides a small return in terms of meat. Also, unless he is dispatched at a young age, rooster meat tends to be on the tough side. Experience has taught me it is not worth the effort. Anyway, besides being impractical, it is definitely not humane.

Roosters are really hard to give away and even harder to sell. One rooster per flock is plenty.   So, the question of what to do with surplus roosters remained unanswered until I saw someone speeding away from a bewildered looking dog they had apparently dropped on the side of the road. If people from town can drop off unwanted dogs and cats in the country, why not roosters? Of course, the difference would be to make it as humane as possible. People drop off dogs and cats and try to convince themselves the animals will find good homes and live a happy life. This rarely happens. But, with some field work and advance planning, it might work for roosters. I began my experiment by driving the narrow country roads in a county to my north specifically searching for places which had chickens roaming freely around the yard and nearby fields. These locations were locked into my brain as possible drop sites. The number of sites selected was based on the number of surplus roosters that had accumulated in my chicken pen. Next, I secured enough of the stiff paper sacks still used in some stores so that each rooster had his own sack.   Common flimsy plastic bags would not work for this operation. When drop day arrived it was necessary to catch the roosters and place one in each paper sack.

My wife hates the next part but she dislikes roosters even more.   By default, she has to be my accomplice.   Her job is to drive to the first drop site, making sure the body of the car shields me from any curious eyes. On some of these roads all eyes are curious because they rarely see a car. If the occupants of the car are acting in a suspicious manner the residents tend to get in their truck and follow you to your destination, fully armed of course. As the car slowly moves past the chickens already in residence, I hold the sack upside down out the window and, presto, the rooster drops to the ground. The perfect scenario would be for the rooster to be welcomed with open arms into the new flock.

However, the reality of the situation sometimes makes it necessary for him to fight the current cock-of-the-walk. If he wins, he reigns supreme. If not, he lives on the fringes of the flock and keeps one eye open for his competition because the resident rooster is prone to launch frequent surprise attacks to chase away the intruder. At least, he is not on the dinner table and that, my friends, is what I call a happy ending for everybody concerned.

The raccoon problem has somewhat of a different history. My shop is frequently a home for cats dropped off by folks that are simply not friendly toward cats, and these people are quite prevalent. A cat can make itself unwelcome by simply having a bad attitude. The presence of a large dog at our house invariably forces the cats to take up residence in the attic of my shop, which provides a warm, dry, secure home. The presence of a cat is also a deterrent to the many squirrels who have also staked a claim to the attic, but the cats always prevail by utilizing the law of the claw and fang. Since the squirrels are unarmed, they return to their rightful home in the trees, where they should have been in the first place. To show my appreciation to the cats, I keep an automatic feeder in the attached shed and the cats enjoy the luxury of an all you can eat buffet. However, other critters, such as raccoons, are frequent interlopers and must be dealt with, hopefully in a humane manner. If allowed to eat freely, the raccoons will dispose of several pounds of feed per night and this rate of consumption is unacceptable because cat food is not given away at the feed store. Not wishing to harm the raccoons, I entice them inside a wire cage-like trap baited with, you guessed it, cat food.

One must be vigilant when dealing with raccoons because they are not the cuddly, furry likeable creatures pictured in cartoons. They are actually very fierce animals and have been known to attack people, sometimes unprovoked. Since I am guilty of provoking them, a great deal of caution is necessary when they are released. Deciding to use the humane approach, I initially took them about a mile away and turned them loose. However, I continued to catch a raccoon almost every night. Talking about this with a friend, he suggested I was trapping the same raccoon every time. If so, the raccoon apparently thought I was running some sort of a federal program to feed hungry critters and was willing to put up with losing his freedom for a few hours for the free meal. To make sure this was not the case, I began using spray paint to make a large blue circle on the back of each one while still in the cage. It would have been extremely difficult, and dangerous, to attempt to spray them after they had been released. At this point the solution to the rooster problem and the solution of the raccoon problem came together nicely with both being transported to the same release point across the state line. Their rooster and raccoon population is growing at a healthy clip. I fully expect to soon hear of a new species of blue-back-raccoon, which has been spotted only in south central Wayne County, near the Natchez Trace. This discovery will certainly necessitate a tax payer funded university grant to study the phenomenon.

What Could Have Been

Our world is full of what could have been or what should have been or what would have been stories. As odd as it may seem, sports fans are experts at reliving the agony of what might have been. The level we experience depends on the amount of winning and losing our favorite team might be going through at the time. There is no problem with being happy to win and sorrowful in defeat. The challenge comes in knowing when to stop agonizing over each defeat to the point we make ourselves, and others, miserable. After a defeat we tend to rehash in our mind all the "what ifs" that caused us to lose. We tell ourselves over and over if they had only done this instead of that we would have won the game. If they had run the ball instead of passing or passed instead of running the outcome would have been different and our happiness would continue for another week. This becomes such an obsession, and I speak chiefly of myself, that enjoying the game, or season, is impossible. This condition seems to run in certain families and it is bothersome to me knowing I have inflicted this disease on my children. Our daughter is a sports fan but is able to deal with defeat much better than her brother. Our son, I fear, is a clone of me at his age. I worry that the ailment is probably incurable in the short run but seems to ameliorate with age. I can only hope they do not allow it to ruin their lives and that my grandchildren are not plagued with the same affliction.

Looking back on a sporting event and bemoaning what should have been done is one thing and can create a lot of good natured fun if not allowed to get out of control. But when a person's life is totally controlled by constantly thinking about what "should have" been, it can become very sad. I am not referring to the daily occurrences where we continually remind ourselves of what we should have done or should not have done. Those things are a part of living and cannot be eliminated.

There are many far more serious things that cause family and friends to become estranged and are allowed to reach the point that they literally dictate what becomes of our life. Sometimes the event causing the separation is so trivial we can't even remember how the problem originated. The Bible tells us in many places to take the initiative to end such quarrels quickly. In no way should they be allowed to take root and spread. Not hating our neighbor is far more than just something we read in the Bible. It should be taken and made a part of how we live our daily lives. The sad part comes when we reach a point in our lives and realize how much better our lives would have been if only we had said one thing or not said another thing and then we begin to go through all the "what ifs" of our life. This picture is made even worse when we realize it is too late to make amends. The situation may be so far out of control and the family so torn, or friendships destroyed, that reconciliation is not possible. Even worse, the person with whom we wish to make things right may no longer be with us. What a tragedy it would be to reach a time and place in life when our physical condition, location, or resources are such that all we are left with is the memory of what we should have done and wishing things could have been different. We rarely get a do-over in life and certainly cannot know when there will be no more opportunities. In all these situations there is no time like the present.

In my own life I wanted for many years to tell my father I loved him but was unable to do so. We had always had a very close relationship and that was not the problem. Expressing my feelings in situations like this has always been very difficult for me, even today.   Neither of my parents were the hugging, emotional type and that was the nature of the household I was raised in.   I suppose it is more difficult to become a hugger if you didn't grow up around huggers. It must have been different with my older siblings because my sister is a world champion hugger. But, I just felt it was important for my dad to hear me tell him that I loved him. So many times I was so close but the opportunity never seemed to be right and when it was right the words just would not come.   As he became older and older, it became evident each chance might be my last. He lived in a small house trailer next to our home for several years and one night before leaving I stopped at his door, turned around and straight out of the blue told him I loved him. The world didn't stop turning, the sky didn't fall and he responded as if I had said it a hundred times. He just looked up from his chair and said, "I love you too." That short exchange was one of the most meaningful of my life with my father. From that point on, it was so easy to say and I could have kicked myself for waiting so long. His health was failing fast and the opportunity would have soon been lost. There is no doubt that I would have been tormented for the remainder of my life telling myself what I should have done. I cannot imagine how I would have felt if he had passed away before I tore down that silly wall. It is a very bad thing when we allow ourselves to become prisoners of our own mind. When we are held captive by our mind we live inside ourselves and nothing else can break through. The children of Israel marched around the city of Jericho for seven straight days before the walls came crashing down. The experience with my father taught me that barriers we put up around ourselves and our loved ones can be breached with a few simple words if we are willing to be the one to take the initiative.

T'was the Day after Christmas

My ability to turn an ordinary event into something resembling a calamity is legendary, at least according to my wife. She delights in regaling friends with some of my exploits that have so far, at least, not been fatal. However, this freedom does have its limits. Some of the predicaments of my own making are so mortifying that she has agreed to hold off telling about them until after my funeral. She graciously agreed to do this at my own request.

One of her favorites, which may be humorous in hindsight, occurred the day after Christmas in the house we were living in at that time. As usual, Christmas produced a mountain of boxes and wrapping paper. Today, disposing of all this paper would not be a problem, it would be sent to recycling. At that time, recycling was not an option. Normally, this paper would have been taken outside and burned but this simple act has, at times, created a great deal of consternation among our neighbors. I will admit that my propensity to resort to outside burning to dispose of unwanted material has created some tense moments among those in the neighborhood with an irrational fear of out of control wildfires. One such time might possibly have been the day I was minding my own business bush hogging our pasture when I ran over an underground nest of bumblebees and was ruthlessly attacked. Trying to escape a swarm of stinging insects of any kind, while driving a tractor, is not recommended and should be avoided at all costs. Finally, I had to shut down my tractor and flee on foot. To avoid making the same mistake again, the nest would have to be eliminated. The best way to do this is to pour gasoline down into the nest cavity. Since the bumblebees were still angrily swarming around the hole in the ground it was necessary for me to attempt this while still trying to avoid more stings. As a result of my haste to get away, the job was sort of half way botched and the survivors were still evident. It was at this point I made a serious error in judgment and decided to finish the job by shooting a flaming arrow into the gasoline from a safe distance, thereby consuming the remaining bumblebees. I fetched my bow, tied a rag around the end of an arrow, poured a little gas on it, set it ablaze and sent it straight to its intended target. My plan worked wonderfully well in solving the bumblebee problem but it had one unintended result. I had not foreseen setting the field ablaze which, unfortunately, did occur. The excitement of watching a fire truck douse a fire brought a stream of cars behind the truck. The fire truck with all the cars looked sort of like a Christmas parade. When their numbers combined with our neighbors who were already watching the spectacle, we had quite a crowd. After the fire truck finally left, I was able to finish mowing without fear of being stung.

So, it was for these reasons that, on this particular day, I decided to simply add the paper to the fire already burning in our fireplace and be done with it. It should be noted here this decision was against the advice of my wife who had developed a keen eye for bad decisions on my part. The problem of creosote build-up in the chimney should have played more of a role in my decision but, unfortunately, I failed to factor it in. For many years I had cut firewood and used this fireplace as a major source of heat for our house, building up a thick layer of this flammable material inside the chimney. The boxes and paper caught up quickly and had almost completely burned up when I remembered something that needed to be done elsewhere. Leaving in my truck, I just happened to glance and look back in my outside mirror. What I saw was very scary. A huge flame, sort of like a Saturn V rocket blasting off, was shooting out the chimney. This caused me to immediately regret my decision to use the fireplace to dispose of the paper and for once wish I had followed my wife's advice. It was at this point that the day took a major turn for the worse. Running back inside I told my wife we had a chimney fire but not to call the fire department, I could take care of it. Why bother those volunteer firemen who are probably at home enjoying the day with their families? Hastily, I ran to the shop, grabbed my ladder and climbed to the roof with a large piece of plywood in my hand. My theory was to cover the chimney, depriving the fire of oxygen and smother it. I had seen this method of putting out a chimney fire on television. Up close, the flame was making a loud, very frightening noise. However, my wife ran out shouting the house was on fire forcing me to quickly change my plans. Scrambling down, I found the house filling with smoke and my wife on the phone with the 911 operator. I told our daughter to ride her bike down the driveway and point the fire truck in the right direction. She misunderstood and thought she had to go all the way to the highway several miles away. Smoke was coming from the receptacles in the sheetrock wall which separated the fireplace from the kitchen. Racing to my shop again, I returned with my wrecking bar and a ten pound hammer. Furiously, I ripped sheetrock from the wall. Then, taking my water hose, I drenched the inside of the wall thinking that to be the source of the fire. The excitement was over by the time the firemen arrived. After studying the mess that was once our living room and kitchen, they reached a startling conclusion. The chimney fire had been put out but the resulting smoke was trapped inside the chimney by the cap I placed on top. Having no place else to go, the smoke began to seep through the porous mortar joints into the wall and escape through the receptacle holes. There had been no fire in the wall or anyplace else, except the chimney. Since there was no fire, I had needlessly destroyed the wall with my wrecking bar and flooded the house with water. Also, our daughter had frantically ridden her bike several miles roundtrip and she was totally exhausted. Other than that, the day had gotten off to a great start.

The moral to this story is never burn paper in a fireplace. Also, pay more attention when your wife gives you good advice.

Some Embarrassing Moments

All of us experience times in our lives when we are extremely embarrassed. Some of these times are of our own making and some are created by others, either intentionally or unintentionally. My life, as my wife will readily attest, has been filled with many such bloopers, mostly the result of my own flawed logic and some just simply by being in the wrong place at the wrong time.   It has been said that the ability and willingness to laugh at ones' self is a sign of maturity and good mental health. I certainly hope that is true because as I get older some of my most entertaining moments are those I spend laughing at some of my blunders, or at least those I can remember.

Early in my teaching career, I was sort of goaded into accepting a leadership position in the local teachers' association. Actually, it was a thankless job nobody else wanted and could easily send your teaching career down in flames if you ticked off the superintendent and the country club crowd that made up the board of education.   Setting aside my common sense, I agreed to take the office thereby launching myself on a path that eventually led me to the state capital and then on to the nation's capital. In addition, it led me to the men's clothing store where I was forced to buy a lot of new clothes. Along the way I was privileged to meet people and was invited into places that would have otherwise never been possible for someone like me.   My decision may have prevented me from being promoted to jobs that I probably wouldn't have liked anyway, but it was worth it. Regardless, it led to some very awkward times in a lot of different places that still make me laugh.

To train local leaders in the fine art of leadership, sessions were scheduled across the state. Soon, after accepting my new position, I attended one such weekend session which was held on a college campus near the geographical center of the state. First on the schedule was a reception followed by dinner on Friday evening, after the participants had registered and checked in.   Let me first confess that my dining out experience had been extremely limited at that time of my life. My parents raised seven children during some lean years and dining out was not even a tiny part of our life.   My father was more interested in providing his family with the necessities of life and he did not consider dining out to be in that category. My first experience with a sit-down restaurant came as a teenager with one of my uncles.

Later on, my wife and I found that raising a family on a teacher's salary did not afford many opportunities to dine out and develop a gourmet appetite. So, I was challenged in this area in ways other than knowing which fork to use. At the reception, the first food item to catch my eye when I entered the cafeteria was boiled shrimp. The shrimp were arrayed around a large ice sculpture. Now, I was not unaware of the existence of shrimp. We had fried shrimp occasionally, taken frozen from a box. But, I had never eaten, or even seen, a boiled shrimp face to face. Eagerly, I loaded my plate, anticipating something new and delicious. Totally oblivious to the fact they had to be peeled before consuming, I chowed down. My first reaction was extreme disappointment. They were not nearly as good as I had been led to believe. In fact, they were far too crunchy which made them difficult to swallow. Praise the Lord for a good friend who slowly peeled his shrimp so that it was impossible for me to miss the obvious. Boiled shrimp is now my favorite seafood, but my embarrassment still lingers to this day.

It seems some of my most flagrant social mishaps occurred when I was attending out of town meetings. One of my worst faux pas occurred several years later in a not to different setting. My involvement at the local level led me to seek a position representing my district on the state teachers' association board of directors. Strangely enough, I was elected, even without having to tamper with the ballots. Soon, it was time to attend my, eagerly awaited, first state board meeting. The board met on the top floor of the headquarters building in the state capital located next door to the famous Dexter Avenue Baptist Church once pastored by Dr. Martin Luther King. We were seated around an incredibly long and massive wooden table which made me feel like I was in a very important place. Shortly before the meeting began, I sought out the restroom, which, I was told was down the hall and around the corner. Turning the corner, I spotted what looked like the word 'men' on a door and entered. The restroom was empty but there were several stalls with doors and I blundered on in. I did notice the absence of any urinals and I was soon to discover the reason. The arrival of some other folks made it painfully obvious I was in the wrong room. The voices and general tone of the conversation quickly gave it away. Surely, someone would sound the alarm and alert my new colleagues that a pervert was loose in the women's restroom. I was positive some of these women carried pepper spray and would not be shy about using it. My rapid ascension to the top of the leadership hierarchy would be shot down in flames. Miraculously, I heard no screams and there was no stampede trying to get out the door. There were no sirens wailing in the distance. Would I be able to escape without being booked and finger printed? I sweated blood and it seemed to take forever until the coast was finally clear. I made a hasty exit and slowly made my way back to the meeting room. No one seemed to be looking askance at me, so maybe my major blunder had gone unnoticed and my reputation remained intact. However, after getting to know some of these people, it would not have surprised me if they had kept the secret to themselves until it was politically expedient to throw me under the bus. A later investigation revealed

154

to me what had happened. Tracing my steps, I ascertained, as I turned the corner, the w-o in women was hidden by the door trim and only the latter part of the word, m-e-n was visible. The only scar from the experience has been recurring nightmares over the years with me being trapped inside a women's restroom. This indicates either the need for serious counseling or the need to face up to a dark side of my personality.

Alas, another more humiliating experience awaited me when my colleagues were gracious enough to continue kicking me up the ladder and elected me to a position on the Board of Directors at the national level. These meetings took place in Washington, D. C., in view of the White House. On more than one occasion, I sat in my hotel room looking out my window at the Washington Monument and actually wondering if a background check would expose me as a fraud. Surely, if they discovered I was from a small rural county school they would be forced to expel me from this august group. Needless to say, being out of my element was frequently on my mind.

The year was 1988, and the nation was celebrating the 200th anniversary of the United States Constitution. The commemoration was to take place in a specially constructed arena in front of the nation's capital. The entire Board of Directors had been invited to sit in the VIP section for this momentous occasion. We were taken by bus with a police escort almost to our seats. The event was covered live by all three national television networks. The President, Supreme Court, Congress, and literally hundreds of dignitaries were in attendance. The event took far longer than it should have but that is the way it always is when so many politicians are present. A couple of hours into the drawn-out festivities, it became necessary for me to visit the restroom. We grew up calling this room, found in many public places, the bathroom, but later realized I never actually saw a bathtub in one. However, I did see one fellow taking sort of a bath in one but that is not pertinent to this story. A nearby usher pointed out dozens of portable toilets, now called port-a-potties, arrayed on a rise which, strangely enough, overlooked the festivities below. Even someone with my background knew enough to make sure the outhouse couldn't be seen from the living room. Making my way up the hill through the crowd, I found a vacant john, locked the door and took a seat. My reverie was interrupted suddenly when the door was violently jerked open, in spite of it being locked. In front of me stood an elderly lady with the door handle in one hand and her purse in the other, apparently unfazed by the lock and the 'occupied' sign showing on the door. Her proximity to me was troubling but not nearly as problematic as the scene I was seeing over her shoulder. Clearly visible was President Reagan speaking at the podium, the Supreme Court seated on risers behind him, and both branches of Congress off to one side. The vexing part was that if I could see them, obviously, they could see me. This situation was totally unacceptable. My words to the elderly lady made me ashamed later, but much, much later. Jerking the door closed, my first question was why do these toilets not have a back door? The second question was have I been spotted by the cameras? This situation was prime material for one of those blooper shows so popular on television. I tried to shield my face as I fled the scene with what little dignity I could muster. The route back to my seat was very circuitous, like a rabbit trying to lose the hounds on his trail and I was constantly glancing back over my shoulder. This is exactly the type behavior the Secret Service is trained to look for because it fits perfectly the profile of a terrorist.

There are three things about this event which should be a lesson. First, never trust the door lock on a portable toilet. Second, keep an eye on elderly ladies when you are engaged in any activity which requires a great deal of privacy. Third, a full moon can occur in the nation's capital during broad daylight.

Driving Jaybo

One of the lessons learned as a school counselor is that none of us know what others go through outside the school house walls. Students come to school hungry, cold, from a friend's house after running away, needing a bath, from an abusive home, straight from jail and all sorts of other dire situations most people could never imagine. The same can be said of folks we come across in everyday life as well. We simply don't know their situation until we walk a mile in their shoes. The daily events inside the guidance office of a high school would provide ample material for a television sitcom. However not everything that goes on is sad, some things are quite funny. At least, they are funny when you look back on them.

A senior at our school, we'll call Jaybo, was a frequent visitor to my office. Not because he constantly needed counseling, but because he was almost twenty years old and had been in high school forever. Teachers would always call on Jaybo to run errands for them because he had already taken their class multiple times and everyone was determined he would get his diploma, or else. Luckily for Jaybo, this was before the state mandated every student had to pass a comprehensive exam before they could graduate. Since he had a lot of free time on his hands, Jaybo was fond of visiting and just talking to anyone who would listen. During the course of one of our conversations, Jaybo revealed he was about to lose his part-time job because his mother could no longer leave her job to take him to and from work. It surprised me that Jaybo did not have a driver's license. He had a permit but said his mother never had the time during the work week to take him for his road test. A plan quickly developed in my mind to help him get his license.

In hindsight, along about here, I missed a red flag. Almost four years had passed since his sixteenth birthday. Since he was almost twenty, this seemed to be a long time for his mother not to find a couple of hours to take him to get his license. It certainly would have relieved a lot of the pressure on her for him to have a license. It also seemed to be unusual since Jaybo had passed our drivers education class when he was sixteen. A second red flag was overlooked when his teacher hesitated before answering "yes" when asked if Jaybo could drive. He should have been interrogated further, but I foolishly let it go. The school principal and Jaybo's mother gave the project their endorsement and the last hurdles had been cleared.

We were going to use my car for the driving test. It was a white, Dodge K car with an anemic four cylinder engine. This prevented anyone from ever being ticketed for speeding, as long as the speed limit did not exceed 25 mph. The big day finally arrived.

Many of the teachers who knew what was going on were really excited for Jaybo. A send off from the school band would not have been a surprise. Since Jaybo was not familiar with my car, it was only logical to let him get some practice on the way to the test center, which, I should mention, was on the other side of the mighty Tennessee River. Reason dictated his driving skills would be somewhat rusty with so little experience.

Leaving school on the two lane residential street made me sit up and take notice. Jaybo drove in the middle of the street, paying no attention to my exhortations to move over or to the angry shouts and surprised looks of the oncoming drivers. Perhaps it wasn't so much that his driving skills were rusty, they were practically nonexistent. The situation worsened when we turned onto the busy four lane road which took us downtown. He seemed confused as to which lane, inside or outside he should drive in, so he just drove in both. He shifted lanes constantly, always suddenly and without warning. This was quite unnerving and made me start to rethink the whole idea. My shouts of "watch out" or "move over" seemed to distract him so I soon learned to keep quiet. But, it was too late to turn back, so we forged ahead. The next major hurdle was the turn onto the busy boulevard leading to the bridge across a very wide river. Jaybo made the turn as if he were driving a tractor in the middle of a large pasture, totally ignoring the traffic as they desperately tried to compensate for his erratic lane changes. Through no fault of his own, he managed to make the turn without hitting anything and was now on a beeline for the bridge. At this point, I would have donned a flotation device if one was available but I don't normally keep one in my car. Details of what actually happened on the bridge are not available because my eyes were closed. However, I could feel the car lurching from one lane to the other as I listened for, and expected to hear the sound of metal tearing and brakes squealing. Clearly pictured in my mind was a Dodge K car, in slow motion, in a free fall into the dark water below. A ridiculous thought came to mind, could Jaybo swim? I soon realized I didn't care. If he took us over the edge, he was on his own. The bridge ordeal seemed to last forever but we made it. After one more major left hand turn, which went about as badly as expected, we pulled into the parking lot of the test center.

The driving test was given at the headquarters of the Alabama Highway Patrol office and there were several patrol cars parked in the lot. Actually, it was a relief not to see any of the officers sprinting to their car to give chase after what I imagined were dozens of reports from raging motorists of a white Dodge heading in their direction with a madman at the wheel. Jaybo had made the trip without an actual mishap but had apparently learned nothing from my earlier shouted instructions. There was soon to be a mishap, however. It occurred when Jaybo and the lady examiner left the parking lot. A right hand turn out of the lot might have been possible and within his extremely limited range of driving skills. The left hand turn, she unwisely insisted Jaybo make, involved navigating through a concrete divider which separated the north and south-bound lanes. The divider is rather easily navigated by steering the car through a very wide opening. Jaybo managed to miss the opening and, from my vantage point in the parking lot, the head of the examiner appeared to make serious contact with the interior roof of the car as it bounced up and over the barrier. Another problem with the left hand turn was that it took them directly into the busiest intersection in the whole area. I can only imagine what happened when they arrived and, thankfully, I heard no collision noises but I could hear the sounds of many horns blowing.

There are times in life when one knows the answer to a question without the question even being asked. I knew there was no need for me to ask, "How did it go?" A few minutes later, the car could be seen returning to the parking lot. The fact that the examiner was now driving answered any questions I might otherwise have asked. She had reached the same conclusion as I had, that Jaybo was a threat to the driving public. The examiner quickly exited the car with the keys in her hand and made a beeline in my direction. Actually, I was hoping she would not recognize me as the idiot who was insane enough to leave him at her door. I realized she was not armed but thought she might hit me. Instead, she made it a point to thrust the keys in my direction and said, somewhat angrily I might add, "Do not let him behind the wheel." The return trip back to school passed quickly, with little conversation.

Several years later, Jaybo came by to visit with his wife and two children. I didn't ask who was driving.

Blessings, Campfires and Dulcimers

As time goes by it is quite obvious that the years behind me far outnumber whatever years are ahead. This makes it a lot easier to reflect on the past than to make definite plans for the future.   People talk about their bucket list and how many things they want to do with whatever time they have left in their lives.   That is fine and dandy but the only bucket that concerns me at this point in my life is the one I try to avoid kicking. For some reason at the turn of every decade of my life it surprises me that I have made it that far. From my teenage years to my sixties I have been somewhat surprised to find myself still alive when each decade rolls around.   Every one of these decades of my life have sort of opened a new chapter and closed the door on another. That may turn out to be one of the keys to enjoying life, knowing when to close one door and allow other doors to open. I have seen some mighty unhappy folks who seem determined not to let another door

The McDonald siblings, known as The Kinfolk, shown on stage at a dulcimer festival in Tullahoma, Tennessee. Left to right is Virginia, John and Tom. Ray Hundley, of Nashville, is playing the guitar.

open as they grow older. But I have found that as stages of my life recede into the past and become a memory the next door that opens has its challenges but the sky didn't fall on my head either.

Following my teens, the challenge was in figuring out how to cope with married life and earn a living while raising a family.   All of a sudden I was in my fifties and the challenge was to adjust to the empty nest and our children living hours away from us. Now life is all about how to grow old with grace and dignity and to avoid embarrassing myself.

161

Growing older has been the most difficult challenge I have ever encountered. I have tried to remember not to resent growing old because many are denied that privilege. It is an often used cliché, but time does fly as you get older. It seems that one day I was twenty-five and the next day I was sixty-five. The last forty years seem like a short walk around the block. One day my mind and body worked together to get things done and now they operate on entirely different schedules. My mind says there's work to do and get on with it. My body says I need a break and we'll start again tomorrow. But there is one undeniable fact about all the years of my life and that is God has blessed me with so many good things they can't be counted. To say that not a single one of these blessings has been deserved doesn't even begin to describe the situation.

There are things that come to us later in life that we never imagined even existed when we were younger. The same can be said of people. I believe God puts certain people in our life for a reason, just as he may put us in someone else's life for a reason. This can be for only a short period of time or for a lifetime.

One of the great blessings that became a big part of my life for a period of time was my love affair with the dulcimer. A dulcimer is a stringed folk instrument made of wood. It is played by placing it in your lap and strumming and has a very mellow sound. Since they are fairly easy to learn to play I was able to fulfill a lifelong goal of learning to play a musical instrument. But the instrument itself was not the real blessing. Along with it came countless people I never would have had the privilege and blessing of knowing if I had not played the dulcimer. It allowed me to spend years of quality time with my brother and sister that enriched all our lives. I encountered my first dulcimer in 1980 at a craft show in the Smoky Mountains. A fellow by the name of Paul Pyle built and sold these instruments. Its sound and simplicity attracted me and the affair began. Along with the dulcimer, he gave me a few basic lessons in how it was to be played. Later, I was to learn that Paul Pyle was one of the most prominent dulcimer makers in the region and was known far and wide for his fine instruments.

Over the years I taught myself how to play and, when he showed a lot of interest, showed my brother Johnny how to strum and fret the instrument. That was the beginning of a great time in all our lives. He was able to take those few rudimentary lessons and, with a lot of discipline and practice, became one of the best players in the area. Within a few weeks he had far surpassed the meager skills it had taken me years to learn. Our sister, who plays by ear, was able to master the dulcimer as she had the piano, without ever taking a lesson. Along with a few friends, we began playing as a folk group and played in many venues in the region.

It was during these years I was privileged to meet some of the finest people I have had the honor of knowing. My brother, Johnny, was far more than a brother, he was my best friend. He showed all of us how to live and die with grace and dignity. He was a great brother to me and a friend to all who knew him. There was such a large crowd at his funeral that people had to be turned away. Johnny taught himself to be a great dulcimer player but his greatest contribution was the life he lived with pain dogging his every step.

Our mutual friend, Hollis Long, of Golden, Mississippi, was a musician and instrument maker in every sense of the word with enough talent to make it big but he wanted nothing to do with that lifestyle. Instead, he lived humbly and walked faithfully with his Creator. Spending time with friends and family gave him the only wealth he wanted out of life. Hollis was always ready to drop whatever he was doing and go somewhere to play music.

Billy Heard from Bitter Branch was a friend to every person he ever met. He was already retired when I met him and camping and playing the dulcimer occupied a great deal of his time. He became sort of an ambassador for the dulcimer and touted its virtues where ever he went. Billy was hard of hearing but he played his dulcimer and sang as if he were performing for royalty. Our campfire music sessions in campgrounds across four states will always be among my most precious memories. Billy and his wife, Eunice, drove the loop in Cades Cove more than any human being who ever lived and enjoyed every trip as if it was their first or maybe their last.

From left, John McDonald, Tom McDonald and Billy Heard perform in the Lynchburg, Tennessee, town square gazebo during the Jack Daniel's birthday celebration.

Horace Eaves of Waterloo was an artist and a craftsman whose work could have been a hit in downtown New York. His paintings, carvings and beautifully crafted dulcimers were the equal of any seen anywhere. The trouble is, very few people ever saw

163

any of his work. I said he was a craftsman, not a salesman. He preferred to live quietly in Waterloo and was probably the most humble man I have ever met.

All of these guys served their country with honor and their lives were guided by their faith. They were not just hearers of the Word they were doers of the Word.   It was impossible for me to be around them without feeling blessed. Their gentleness, kindness, sense of humor and love for their fellow man and country left a lasting impression on everyone they met.   I know that God put them in my life for a reason and I hope enough of their genuineness rubbed off on me to make a difference. It was an honor for me to know them and to play music with them for a time that was cut short by sickness and death.

Fire Trucks and Orange Crush

Volunteer fire departments scattered across this nation provide a great service to those of us living in rural areas. Those who give of their time in such a worthwhile endeavor are to be commended. They not only save lives and property but their presence in any given area results in much lower rates on home owners insurance. We experienced these benefits when the department several miles away decided to build a satellite station very close to our house.

The local fire chief at that time owned the community general store and we spent a lot of time talking on my frequent visits to purchase items needed around the place. On one such visit, he mentioned that the tanker truck in the new station was often not taken to fires because of a driver shortage. Most rural areas either don't have fire hydrants or enough hose to reach one that might be more than a mile away. The tanker trucks are essential to haul water to the fires without a nearby hydrant. Many homes have burned to the ground with fire trucks around it because there was not enough water available. The news he gave me that day was disturbing so I volunteered to help when needed. It would be an absolute nightmare for fireman to have to stand around and watch a home burn because no one was available to bring water to the fire. However, it was made clear to the chief that my proposal did not include hauling hose and ladders and dashing into burning buildings. I had no desire whatsoever to be a real fireman. Volunteering to drive the tanker truck, when no one else was available, was the extent of my offer. To be allowed to drive any emergency vehicle it would be necessary for me to go through the licensing course offered by the state agency representing volunteer fire departments. The two day session had already been scheduled to take place in a few weeks and my name was added to the list.

The first day of training was held at the local fire station. The state had sent an instructor to conduct the course. We viewed videos and studied state law regarding the operation of emergency vehicles and any possible liability involved. The actual driving took place on the second day. We were required to drive a tanker truck through a course laid out on the parking lot of the local school. Two trucks were available. One was a recently purchased newer model that actually looked like a real fire truck. The other was an older U. S. Army troop carrier which had been converted into a tanker truck and looked as if the metal salvage yard might be somewhere in its near future. The luck of the draw put me in the old military vehicle for my driving test. I could readily see the first problem I would encounter with the driving portion of the test would be to actually get myself up into the cab of the truck. The first step appeared to be about three feet from the ground and I would have to stand on an apple crate to make it. However, there was another problem with the older truck that would normally require a great deal of getting used to.

Extreme usage over the years, probably jumping hedgerows in France during WWII, had caused excessive wear in the steering system. The wheel could be turned almost 360 degrees before the worn out linkage would cause the front wheels to respond to the driver's attempt to turn and it was impossible to predict when this response might occur without considerable practice. Practice time was not part of the instructor's agenda for the day. The driving course had been marked by using small orange cones. Running out of cones, the instructor had purchased about a dozen three liter plastic bottles of orange soda to complete the course layout. Our test involved successfully keeping the truck between the cones as we drove straight ahead about 75 yards and then in reverse back to the starting point. That part was no problem. Then we had to drive forward through a winding, serpentine course, staying between the cones and then the same pattern in reverse. My problems began with the reverse portion. Using only mirrors, it was difficult to judge the distance the rear wheels were from the cones. This was a critical factor when trying to decide when to begin turning the unpredictable steering wheel. As I moved backward, I could clearly see that the rear wheels were drifting toward the cones because the wheel was not responding properly. Misjudging the steering as the curve turned in the other direction placed the giant rear wheels of the truck on top of the soda bottles.

The first bottle exploded in a giant orange boom, splashing some of the liquid onto the mirror on my side. Stopping and pulling forward to readjust the wheels was not allowed, so I had no choice but to continue. Every few feet the truck traveled, another bottle exploded creating a giant orange geyser until all twelve had been mashed flat, giving the asphalt a distinctly orange tint. During the series of explosions, the examiner sat stoically in the seat beside me, marking something on his clipboard. Attempting to inject some humor into an awkward situation, I remarked that I had seen many fires but had never come across one with any cones set up for the trucks to back through and jokingly asked who was responsible for cone placement. If they couldn't use my services as a driver maybe I could get that job. Sometimes I ask stupid questions when I am embarrassed and this situation fit the bill perfectly. He apparently did not think my ill-timed comment was funny but he did give me a passing grade. Apparently his scoring system was tilted in such a manner that more points were awarded for the driving forward portion of the test than the driving in reverse portion. Also, there is a small chance he gave me additional credit for having a perfect score on the drink bottles, twelve for twelve.

Before we parted company, I made what I thought was a generous gesture to pay for the orange drinks but he said the state association paid his expenses. I wondered later how his supervisor reacted to his expense voucher for this trip listing mileage, lodging, meals and twelve three liter bottles of orange drink. But who knows, this might be happening all over the state and I may have set a new state record.   Unless the association treasury has more money than it knows what to do with, it might be cheaper in the long run to invest in more cones.

Economics 101

Growing up as a kid in the 1950's, I had very little knowledge about how to handle money. This can be explained by the simple fact that I never had any money to handle. Therefore, any knowledge I might have had about handling money was theoretical, based on no valid experience whatsoever. This problem was not unique with me but was shared by every kid I knew. Not only was actual cash money scarce for kids, the adults in our neighborhood didn't seem to have much of it either. This predicament made it necessary to use ingenuity and what little sense we had to devise ways to rectify the situation.

There was a real scarcity of opportunity to put money in your pocket in those days. Jobs for kids were virtually non-existent. Today, there are many low paying jobs for young people in the fast food industry or working in retail. Some have even established their own business by mowing lawns. Fast food can be quickly ruled out because there were no such businesses at that time. Mowing lawns was not feasible because we didn't own a lawnmower. We cut our yard with a reel mower, which means without a motor, which had blades about as sharp as a broom handle. Weeds too high to bruise and cripple with the reel mower were attacked with a sling blade. For those who don't know, a sling blade is an instrument apparently salvaged from the depths of a torture chamber. It was used primarily on young boys in an attempt to encourage them to run away from home and leave town with the carnival. I have two sling blades in my possession, both hanging on my wall like a prized deer head.

Another potential source of income that had to be quickly eliminated, along with fast food establishments and mowing grass, would be working for my daddy. He believed strongly that if he fed you and clothed you and gave you a place to sleep at night he had no obligation to pay you for any work that he might assign you to do. This was a policy he developed from the beginning and closely followed until the very end. In addition to not paying, he was too quick to loan out his boys to neighbors who were in need of cheap labor. Personally, I have unloaded sand, dirt, and gravel, cleaned up old bricks and lumber, ran errands and much more for little more than a thank you. My brothers suffered the same fate. Some states have passed laws preventing convicts from being treated in this manner. Much later in life, my daddy shared some sage advice with me as far as whom not to hire to work for you. First, never hire anyone who rolls his own cigarettes. His reasoning was that the person would spend more time rolling his cigarettes than working. Second, never hire a man who wears gloves when he works. Again, he reasoned the fellow would spend more time looking for his gloves than he would spend working. Since he had experience in that area, who was I to disagree?

However, there was a small entrepreneurial window open to kids but it required a great deal of work. There was a good business in recapping old tires and selling them to people who could not afford new tires for their vehicle. Daddy probably bought more recaps than cigars, and he was a big cigar man. The closest recapping place when I was a kid was in downtown Florence, across from Pope's Tavern. They were willing to pay the whopping price of one thin dime for any tire in good enough condition to recap. To take advantage of this opportunity, one had to first locate an acceptable tire and second, deliver it to the recapping man. Old tires were not that hard to find. Discards were frequently found in ditches at the bottom of a hill. They wound up in a ditch because they had probably been used to roll around for fun by a kid who lived on top of the hill and was too lazy to fetch it when it got away from him and rolled down the hill. Transporting the tire to the recapping place was a big problem and caused many kids to shut down their business.

Rolling a tire a short distance is kind of fun. Rolling a tire about two miles is far from fun. Also, a kid cannot walk and roll a tire. In order to remain upright, the tire has to move along at a pretty good clip. This pace is faster than a kid can walk. Therefore, the one rolling the tire has to at least trot to keep pace. Leaving my house, the first mile and a half were fairly flat but hills had to be negotiated toward the end of the trip. Once, I had the bright idea of placing the tire in a wagon and towing it with my bike. That turned out to be much more strenuous than rolling it. When one finally arrived, exhausted, at the recapping place, the tire was given a good once-over to make sure it had no holes. On more than one occasion, my tire was rejected and I rolled it back home and made sure it was left in a ditch for the next enterprising kid. Many old tires probably made the trip downtown several times. Once he was satisfied with the tire, the man paid out the dime.

Herein, lies a good lesson in discipline, plus some understanding of basic economic principles. The city buses ran from downtown to about one block from our house in East Florence. The fare for the bus ride back to the house was one dime. After an exhausting trip rolling a tire all the way to town, it was very difficult to resist the temptation to ride the bus back home. On more than one occasion the enticement was more than I could overcome. It was quite a relief to learn many years later that I wasn't the only kid to succumb to the temptation to ride the bus back home. As a matter of fact, my brother Bobby confessed he had done the same thing. I was to learn in a college economics course that this practice was not recommended and would never result in a profit. A zero profit margin was not sufficient for a business to survive. Perhaps the fact that I engaged in shoddy business practices may help explain why I never had any money.

According to news reports it is very difficult for a small business to succeed. Most close their doors after only a short time. This was exactly what happened to another fledgling business I dabbled in very briefly. Years ago it was not difficult to find scrap metal alongside roads and in areas where people created their own private dump. I decided to salvage small metal pieces and collect them at home until my stash was large enough to sell. There was an old fellow on the hill above us who paid a few cents a pound for scrap metal and would come around to collect it in his old, dilapidated truck. This was very convenient for a kid because transporting a pile of heavy metal was out of the question. When my pile of metal was sufficiently large, I went by his house on my bike and he agreed to come to the house and look it over. He bought the pile for a dollar or so and was about to leave when he spotted a pile of three inch pipe my daddy had brought home years ago. I was not privy to the fact they were intended to use to support a shed he was planning to build. My thinking was that Daddy would be proud of his son for his astute business sense, so I sold the expensive metal pipes for a couple of dollars. Little did I know the deal the old fellow had put off on me was almost as good as the twenty-four dollars in trinkets Peter Minuit paid the Native Americans for Manhattan a couple of hundred years earlier. It would be an understatement to say that my daddy was not impressed at all. After he finished raking me over the coals, he had a few choice words for the old fellow and, as I recall, referred to him as "worse than a thief." After insisting that I accompany him to refund the money and help load the pipe to bring back to the house, he dissolved my small business on the spot. As Barney Fyfe would have said, "Andy, you have got to nip it in the bud," and that is exactly what happened. My daddy was not known for taking a long time to make up his mind. After what Wall Street would describe today as a, "hostile takeover" of my business enterprise, I resorted to selling empty drink bottles and old tires for several more years.

Later, when I had my driver's license, my daddy was able to get me a pretty good part-time job working in the cafeteria at TVA, where he was employed as a carpenter. Early in his administration, President John Kennedy created the Peace Corp, which exists to this very day. The legislation creating this organization was historic and ground breaking. The TVA facilities in Muscle Shoals were chosen as a training site for one of the first groups of Peace Corp volunteers ever assembled. They were fed at the TVA cafeteria. Since Daddy was a good friend with the manager of the cafeteria, he hired me to come in after school and on weekends to wash dishes and clean up the dining room because he was responsible for feeding several hundred more people for the duration of the training. Every weekday after school, I rushed home to change clothes and be at work by four o'clock. My duties involved washing all the large pots and pans by hand, running utensils through the dishwasher and sweeping and mopping the floors after everyone was served. It was usually after ten o'clock before I got home. Child labor laws would prohibit working those hours during the week today but it was not a problem in the early 1960's. The money was a lot better than selling old tires. Besides, I was sort of like a fly on the wall and was privileged to observe first-hand as history making legislation got off the ground.

My point here is not what my duties were on this job, or what my salary was working in the cafeteria as a busboy. During the time I spent there, I was able to observe something totally out of context with everything my sixteen brief years growing up in the Deep South had led me to believe to be true. These Peace Corp volunteers had been assembled from all over the United States. They were male and female and black and white. From the business end of a mop and broom I was able to observe for the first time in my life white folks and black folks mingling together as equals. As the teen-age boy mopping the floor late at night while they finished eating, I was all but invisible to them. I didn't have to eavesdrop because I was right in the middle of their conversations. There was no reason for any of them to pretend or perpetuate a false impression. This was important because it got me to thinking that, just maybe, many of the things I had observed up to this point in my life regarding race were wrong.

Desperate Measures

The 1950's were really a neat time to be a kid. Without going into a great deal of detail, probably the real reason was that our lives were not micromanaged by adults. We played together without supervision and were left to our own devices to create activities to occupy our time. For the most part we roamed near and far and our survival rate was surprisingly high considering all the dire possibilities. Disagreements were settled by a fight which generally ground to a halt due to lack of interest or exhaustion. There is no doubt that this kind of existence would not be possible today. The world is now spinning on a different axis and I fear the kids of this modern world have missed out on an important part of growing up.

However, not all the activities we engaged in were pure or, more importantly, known to our parents. Boys have always had some kind of fascination with using tobacco in one form or another, smoking and chewing being the most common. It was not like we thought up all this stuff by ourselves because we had plenty of adult role models. My father smoked King Edward cigars and a pipe, my mother dipped Bruton snuff, my grandfather chewed Red Man tobacco and all my brothers, with one exception, smoked cigarettes. This is not to mention all the cousins, uncles, and neighbors who fired up a smoke on a regular basis. My father drove us kids around in his old Packard while he puffed on a King Edward that turned the air blue with noxious smoke. Meanwhile, my grandfather, Pa Mac, was sitting in the front passenger seat spitting giant globs of slimy tobacco juice out the window. The old Packard was painted sort of an off white at the factory but it had become a two-tone brown on the passenger side thanks to gallons of Red Man by-product. This practice made it very hazardous and unsanitary for kids in the backseat to enjoy the breeze from windows rolled down, which was our only available air conditioner. This was before the Surgeon General decided cigarettes and tobacco in general, were bad for your health and forced the tobacco companies to print warnings on every pack they produced. In spite of being surrounded by tobacco products and those who used them, it was not all that easy for a ten year old kid and his outlaw friends to maintain a steady supply of cigarettes, or smokes as we called them. However, it was not an impossible task and I am comfortable at this stage of my life to reveal how that was actually accomplished.

A perfectly legitimate way was to purchase them but money was the only problem. Kids rarely had money and, for that matter, neither did many adults. My brother, Johnny, who was a couple years older and a lot smarter than me, came up with a method which was, at best, unethical. Our father doled out a dime to each of us to put in the collection plate on Sunday. Since he never attended church with us, how was he to know we diverted it for other purposes? A pack of cigarettes cost about twenty-five cents at the time. If we forgot to donate the dimes at church and, instead, put them together with a few cents from the pocket of one of our lowlife friends, presto, we had a pack of unfiltered Camels. Only sissies smoked filtered cigarettes. Johnny was also generous enough to let me go inside to make the actual purchase. His reasoning was it would be good experience for me to conduct business transactions on my own without his help.   I suspect the real reason was to provide cover just in case our daddy came along asking questions about who actually purchased the cigarettes?

There was another cheaper method of cigarette procurement but it was distasteful and gross at best and certainly did not promote a healthy lifestyle. This method was only useful during the summer when school did not keep us from monitoring the employees break time at the closest knitting mill in the community. The Sweetwater Knitting Mill had a very loud steam whistle which sounded several times a day. The first came at 8 a.m. when it summoned the employees to work. It blew again at 10 a.m. for the morning break. At 12 noon it sounded for lunch, at 2 p.m. for afternoon break and, lastly, at 4 p.m. for quitting time. Since it was extremely dangerous for the employees to smoke inside a building where the air, and their lungs, was filled with highly flammable cotton fibers, they were allowed to go outside twice a day for a smoke break. During this break time was when the local street urchins began to gather on the front porch of the little store across the road.   Incidentally, this very store was our main supplier when we had the funds with which to actually purchase cigarettes. The merchant unknowingly abetted us in raising funds for this purpose when we occasionally pilfered empty drink bottles he carelessly stored out behind his building and then brought them back into the front door where he gave us two cents each for his own bottles. This was a cash cow we learned to use sparingly lest he become suspicious and begin to keep a closer watch on his inventory out back. We were lined up like buzzards on a fence waiting patiently for the right moment. The mill workers had to quickly discard their partially smoked cigarettes when summoned back inside. When they were all back indoors, we made our move. It was not unusual to retrieve nearly whole cigarettes and many others of varying lengths. Our method of removing deadly germs or other litter was to simply blow on it to remove the contaminants and stick it in our pocket. This method was effective but somewhat desperate.

Lastly, if all else failed, we could revert to going to any of the nearby wooded areas and look for dried honeysuckle vines or rabbit tobacco. The vines were broken into cigarette size lengths and fired up at one end. Since the middle was hollow it was like sucking on a blow torch and one vine went a long way. The weed we called rabbit tobacco was very common. It was crushed and rolled inside newspaper to resemble a real cigarette. If one could ignore the acrid smoke and bitter taste, it wasn't too bad but only if the inside of your mouth had been seared by the fire from the honeysuckle vine.

Kids of my age had a system of sharing such items that was handed down by our older siblings. We didn't invent it we just carried it forward because everyone else did. The words we used at that time have vastly different meanings today. For example, if one person had a cigarette and his friend wanted a puff, he would say, "Let me have a drag off that fag." He was simply asking his friend to share the cigarette. The Merriam-Webster Dictionary actually lists one meaning of drag as "to puff" and fag as a cigarette. So, in reality, this phrase is correct but has a drastically different meaning today and would be wildly politically incorrect. Can you imagine how that phrase would go over in a crowd of yuppies today?

Another peculiar way to ask for a share of something was to use the word, "bootie." For example, if you had the money to buy a soft drink, which we universally referred to as a 'coke,' no matter what was on the label, before you opened it you had to be quick on your toes and say, "no booties." This effectively prevented any of your mooching friends from asking for a swig, sip, or gulp. However, if you failed to utter the word in time, anyone in your group could claim 'booties" and the owner of the treat would be obligated to share with that one individual. This same arrangement could also be used when lusting for a bite from a Moon Pie or other such sweet delicacy. However, this was not a perfect system and problems arose when an excessive bite, sip, swig, or gulp was taken by the moocher. It was not unusual for fisticuffs to break out. Somehow the word "bootie" has taken on an entirely different connotation today and it would be extremely unwise to use that phrase in the wrong crowd, such as a singles bar or in an e-mail to a close friend. In addition, Messrs. Merriam and Webster, dictionary publishers since 1831, remain silent to this very day on the actual definition of the word.

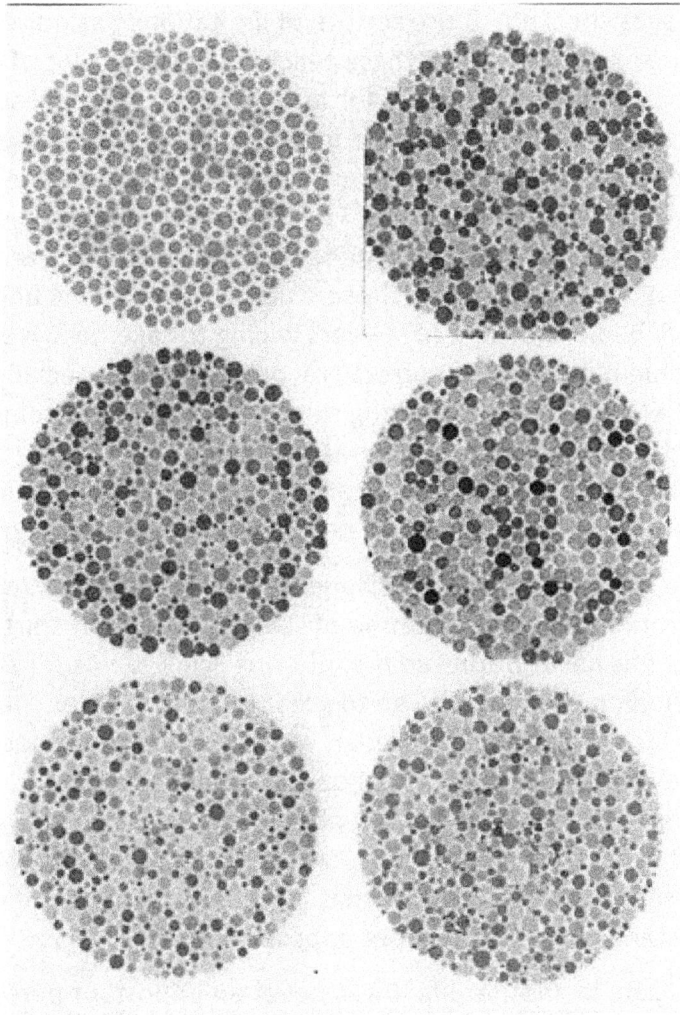

What Color is that?

I was born and raised color-blind and had no clue until I was in college and began to apply for jobs, which required an eye exam. However, looking back on my childhood, there were certain clues that even my teachers overlooked. Coloring is a major part of early elementary school and my ability to place the right color on the right objects caused many of my teachers to write cryptic notes on my art work. These notes generally expressed some degree of puzzlement about my odd sense of color selection. Some were as cold and heartless as to actually deduct points from my report card, but no note to my parents to have my eyes checked. If the statute of limitations has not expired, perhaps it is not too late to bring a lawsuit against these teachers. Today, a lot of folks seem to favor litigation as a way to establish a scapegoat for many of their personal shortcomings. Maybe a case could be made that the callous indifference by my teachers toward my handicap undoubtedly caused me to suffer through bouts of low self-esteem. We can't allow anyone to have low self-esteem. Also, I believe my mediocre grade in college in an art appreciation class could also be laid at the feet of my teachers. Perhaps schools should be forced to provide aides and tutors for those students affected by being color-blind. There would certainly be no shortage of lawyers willing to take my case. On a more serious note, my problem picking out correct crayons became especially severe when the crayons lost their label and I was left to using only eyesight to determine the actual color. The sky was frequently colored purple and grass colored brown during these embarrassing lapses. However, when the label was still attached and I learned to read well enough to pick up on it, there was usually no problem, except later on with my clothes.

Picking the right color clothes has plagued me all of my life. Well, not actually me, but some of those around me. The dilemma of selecting the right shirt to go with the right pants and socks has never bothered me, not one scintilla. As for shoes and a belt, you have got to be kidding. People who go to great lengths to color coordinate their clothes should get a life, or a hobby. However, while this has never been a problem for me, it does bother my wife, not just a little, but apparently a whole lot. When I emerge from my closet having haphazardly thrown together my wardrobe for whatever occasion is at hand, she uses her favorite three words, "Are you blind?" Followed by, "There is no way I'm going to be seen with you wearing that." This less than gentle critique is then followed by her assistance in selecting more appropriate attire.

Several years ago, in another life, I was never an important person, but, somehow, I wound up holding some important positions within my professional association. Consequently, I had to attend a lot of meetings out of town where blue jeans and a sweat shirt were not the preferred mode of dress. Since my wife could not always travel with me and select my clothes, this created somewhat of a quandary for her. I suppose having me appear in front of hundreds of people dressed like Bozo the Clown was a reflection on her choice of a mate and that could not be tolerated. However, she was not to be deterred. Before my clothes were packed, all the outer apparel had a number on a piece of tape attached to the garment. From this you can quickly ascertain she trusted me to pick my own underwear. All I had to do was match up the numbers. If one item could be worn with more than one piece, it had all the appropriate numbers on the tape. This system seemed to work rather well, at least to the point I wasn't publically ridiculed.

178

The question has often passed through my mind as to who thought of all of these ridiculous rules about clothing and colors? Somewhere, back in the dark ages, somebody with a lot of spare time had to come up with which colors matched and which clashed. Inside the cave, the women were sorting through piles of different color animal skins and deciding sabre-tooth tiger skins clash with zebra hides and that hideous, spotted cheetah skin was fit only for trailer trash, whatever that meant. Meanwhile, the men, who were oblivious to the life altering decisions being made inside, simply hunkered around the fire and scratched and spit while trying to figure out an easier way to start a fire. To me, it is simply a matter of opinion.

Today, when someone discovers I am color blind, the first question, while pointing to a nearby object, is always, "What color is that?" People are fascinated when they discover my plight and cannot imagine anyone going through life with this handicap. Most folks immediately think a person affected with this condition sees no color at all. This is not true. The term color-blind is actually very misleading and even downright inaccurate in most cases. Being blind to color would seem to indicate a person is not capable of seeing objects in color. The term color challenged is much more accurate. I can see color but most of the time I just don't know which colors I happen to be seeing. Fall colors are beautiful but just don't ask me to identify the color of the leaves. Color blindness generally affects males much more often than females. The most frequent form is difficulty identifying shades of colors like red or green. The truly rare form does involve a small percentage of people who see in only different shades of gray. I have taken dozens of tests where a mass of different colored dots is displayed with a letter or number hidden inside colored so that only color blind individuals cannot see it. The question is then asked, what letter, or number do you see? I have never seen anything and cannot see it even when someone outlines it for me. To me, it is all much ado about nothing and could possibly even be a hoax.

There have been a few situations in my life where this condition really was a problem and could have been serious. During the early 1960's, when I turned sixteen and got my driver's license, there was a skating rink in Spring Park, located in downtown Tuscumbia. This is a vivid reminder that there really wasn't anything to do around here back in those days. We either went skating on Saturday night, cruised up and down Court Street or went out to Wilson Dam and hoped to see a string of barges lock through the dam. To say there was a vacuum of suitable activities for young people is an understatement. To get to the skating rink, one had to travel right through downtown Tuscumbia. My first trip through town, after I got my license, was a potential disaster in the making. First, the traffic lights were in reverse order. The green light was on top and the red light was on bottom.   Up to this point in my young driving career, my policy was to proceed when the bottom light came on and stop when the top light came on. To me, the color was insignificant; it was location that was important. This was a very simple policy and would have worked in virtually every city in the United States, except Tuscumbia. It also would have worked with anybody who was not color blind. Maybe the city fathers in Tuscumbia felt this was a good way to express their individuality. The other problem was that the traffic lights were located at the corners of the intersection, not hung in the middle as in most places. According to my friends, I ran every traffic light in town on my way to the skating rink. Since I never actually saw a traffic light, they may have been telling the truth. At some point later on, the problem was corrected which allowed me to return to beautiful downtown Tuscumbia and drive normally through intersections without fear of being blind-sided.

There were two situations in which this condition affected employment. The first was when I was in college and was hired to work for the Office of Agricultural Stabilization and Conservation under the auspices of the United States Department of Agriculture. Simply put, I was hired to measure and plot cotton fields on large aerial photographs which were then used to determine actual acreage planted. Each cotton farmer was allotted a specific number of acres to plant in order to keep the price of cotton stable and high enough to make a profit. Fields which exceeded the amount allotted had to be plowed up.   This was a problem for me because the fields had to be measured with a long tape and then drawn to scale with different colored pencils on the aerial photo. Each color represented something vital to the process. Using the wrong color created a problem the government bureaucracy could not handle. It seems that the machines used to read the tracings could not decipher a cotton patch planted where the color on the photo indicated nothing but acres of trees. After I retired from the education profession, I worked for the United States Census Bureau. We were told constantly to, "Think outside the box." The Department of Agriculture would have been better off had they adopted this more open-minded policy.

While in college, a friend's father used his influence to get me a summer job at Reynolds Metal Company. This was the job of a lifetime for me because wages and benefits far exceeded anything I had ever experienced. Initially, I was hired to work in an air-conditioned lab to test the purity of the aluminum by observing the color of the flame as samples were heated to several hundred degrees. Since I could not determine the color of the flame, which was the crux of the job, I was transferred immediately to a furnace tending job in the caste house, which was behind only Hell and the pot room on the list of very hot places you don't want to be. My new job was to stand in front of a twelve hundred degree furnace of molten aluminum and use a long pole to scrape impurities off the top. I never actually visited the pot room but I knew people who worked there and it was described to me as a place of unbearable heat and an inferno of pots of molten aluminum and flames. The friend who described it to me was very good with words. Believe it or not, my job in the caste house turned out to be very educational for me in that it convinced me beyond a shadow of a doubt that I should return to college for a degree. Working straight midnight shifts in the caste house resulted in a change in my attitude without having to serve time in jail.

Many times people give me directions and use color as a focal point. For example, if you are waiting for me to pick you up at your house and my directions are, "Just turn right at the corner and I live in the only green house on the next block," be prepared to wait a while. "Would you please hand me that mauve purse?" is always a head scratcher for someone who is color-blind. People who use words like, lavender, teal, slate, and charcoal are speaking a foreign language to those of us who are color challenged. I have been told that the twelve or so colors most people recognize can be combined and shaded lighter or darker to total millions of different colors. As far as I am concerned, that is all a "pigment" of somebody's imagination.

About the Author

Tom McDonald is the youngest of seven children born to William Ervin and Pauline Lindsey McDonald. He spent his boyhood and part of his teenage years living in the East Florence community. Almost his entire family, parents, grandparents, brothers, sister, aunts, uncles and most cousins attended Brandon Elementary School. Mr. McDonald met his future wife, Margo Wilson, while both were students at Central High School. They were married in 1965 and have two children, Amy and Will. Mr. McDonald received his B.S. degree from the University of North Alabama and his M. A. and Ed. S. degrees from the University of Alabama in Tuscaloosa. He retired from the Florence City School system as a counselor at Bradshaw High School. His hobbies include woodworking and day-hiking on the Appalachian Trail. Mr. McDonald resides with his wife near the Cloverdale Community in rural Lauderdale County in northwest Alabama.

Bluewater Publications is a multi-faceted publishing company capable of meeting all of your reading and publishing needs. Our two-fold aim is to:

1) Provide the market with educationally enlightening and inspiring research and reading materials.
2) Make the opportunity of being published available to any author and or researcher who desire to be published.

We are passionate about preserving history; whether through the re-publishing of an out-of-print classic, or by publishing the research of historians and genealogists. Bluewater Publications is the *Peoples' Choice Publisher*.

For company information or information about how you can be published through Bluewater Publications, please visit:

www.BluewaterPublications.com

Also check Amazon.com to purchase any of the books that we publish.

Confidently Preserving Our Past,
Bluewater Publications.com

www.ingramcontent.com/pod-product-compliance
Lightning Source LLC
LaVergne TN
LVHW061331060426
835512LV00013B/2606